OUT OF JOINT AND THE ROYAL COURT THEATRE PRESENT

O GO MY MAN

BY STELLA FEEHILY

out of joint

Supported by Jerwood New Playwrights

J ERWOOD
CHARITABLE FOUNDATION

First performance at Royal Court Theatre, London, on 12 January 2006

O GO MY MAN

TOUR DATES 2006

12 Jan – 11 Feb
Royal Court Theatre, London
020 7565 5000
www.royalcourttheatre.com

14 – 18 Feb
Cambridge Arts Theatre
01223 503333
www.cambridgeartstheatre.com

21 – 25 Feb
Nuffield Theatre, Southampton
023 8067 1771
www.nuffieldtheatre.co.uk

28 Feb – 4 March
Birmingham Repertory Theatre
0121 236 4455
www.birmingham-rep.co.uk

7 – 11 March
Everyman Palace Theatre, Cork
+353 (0)21 450 1673
www.everymanpalace.com

14 & 15 March
Gardner Arts Centre, Brighton
01273 685861
www.gardnerarts.co.uk

17 & 18 March
Trinity Theatre, Tunbridge Wells
01892 678 678
www.trinitytheatre.net

21 – 25 March
Yvonne Arnaud Theatre, Guildford
01483 44 00 00
www.yvonne-arnaud.co.uk

28 March – 1 April
Octagon Theatre, Bolton
01204 520661
www.octagonbolton.co.uk

Hasselblad Camera by Hasselblad UK Ltd, Contax G2 Camera by Alpha Digital Services, Satellite Phone by Applied Satellite Technology, Broadcast Camera by Metro Broadcast, Soho, Photography Equipment by Jessops Ltd

Thanks to: Silverprint www.silverprint.co.uk, Thames And Hudson, Sage Publications, Morrison Hotel, Dublin, London Communications, Bethan Walters, Film Medical Services Limited, Panavision, Lewis Photos, AMT Coffee (UK) Ltd, Oxford Stage Company, Concord Institute, Pro-Active Ltd, Fabulous Bakin' Boys, Carter-Voce Access Control Ltd, Objective Team Ltd, Mantaya UK Ltd

O GO MY MAN

BY STELLA FEEHILY

Cast

Denise Gough	Elsa
Sam Graham	A Director / Jim / Freddy / Reg / An Ex-Sergeant / The White Rabbit
Paul Hickey	Ian
Susan Lynch	Sarah
Aoife McMahon	Zoe
Gemma Reeves	Maggie
Mossie Smith	Alice / The Queen of Hearts
Ewan Stewart	Neil

Director	Max Stafford-Clark
Set Designer	Es Devlin
Costume Designer	Emma Williams
Lighting Designer	Johanna Town
Sound Designer	Gareth Fry
Music by	Felix Cross
Assistant Director	Naomi Jones

Company Stage Manager	Graham Michael
Deputy Stage Manager	Richard Llewelyn
Assistant Stage Manager	Helen Bowen
Dialect Coach	Jeannette Nelson
Production Electrician	Tim Bray
Production Sound	Caroline Downing
Publicity image and tour print design	Iain Lanyon
Production photography	John Haynes
Set built by	Miraculous Engineering
Costume Supervisors (Royal Court)	Iona Kenrick, Jackie Orton

For Out of Joint

Producer	Graham Cowley
Marketing Manager	Jon Bradfield
Administration and Education Manager	Natasha Ockrent
Production Manager	Gary Beestone

For the Royal Court

Press	Ewan Thomson
Education	Ola Animashawun
Production Manager	Paul Handley

THE COMPANY

DENISE GOUGH

Theatre includes *As You Like It* and *By the Bog of Cats* (Wyndhams, West End); *The Kindness of Strangers* (Liverpool Everyman); *Robber* (Tristan Bates Theatre); *Theatre Train; Fear And Misery In The Third Reich*. **Television** includes *Casualty* and *Tell Me Lies*.

SAM GRAHAM

Sam was in *The Permanent Way* for **Out of Joint** (National Theatre co-production). Previous appearances at the **Royal Court** include *All Things Nice*, and *Conquest of the South Pole* and *Dead Dad Dog* (Royal Court/Traverse). Other **theatre** includes

Normal, Love You, Too (Bush Theatre); *A Month In The Country, Troilus And Cressida, Richard III* (RSC); *Shining Souls* (Old Vic); *Poor Superman* (Manchester Royal Exchange, Best Actor Manchester Evening News Awards); title role in *Macbeth* (Chester Gateway); *Brilliant Traces* (Tron/Traverse); *As You Like It* (Cheek by Jowl); *Love's Labour's Lost, Triumph Of Love, Cloud Nine, Summerfolk* (Chichester Festival Theatre); *Of Mice and Men* (Liverpool Playhouse); *The Prowler* (Traverse); *Loot* (Druid Theatre Company). **Television** includes regular characters D.S. Gary Hunt in *Doctors*, and Archie Malloch in *Footballers' Wives* (Series 1 & 2). Also: *A Good Murder, Fingersmith, Courtroom – Case 0021, Caught In The Wheels, Tipping The Velvet, A & E, Holby City, Monarch Of The Glen II & III, Big Bad World, Kavanagh QC, The Creatives, Maisie Raine, The Professionals, Keeping Mum, A Mug's Game, For Valour, Preston Front* and *All Quiet On The Preston Front, A Touch Of Frost, Making Waves, Forever Green, Taggart* and *Bergerac*. He has also narrated many documentaries for the Discovery Channel. **Film** includes *Karmic Cowboys, Ashes & Sand, The Final Warning* and *Heavenly Pursuits*. **Radio** includes *One Day, Julie And The Prince, The Permanent Way, England Their England, The Red Headed League, Smart Boy Wanted* and *Antony and Cleopatra*.

PAUL HICKEY

Previous appearances at the **Royal Court** include *Fewer Emergencies, Crazyblackmuthafuckin'self*. Other **theatre** includes *The Playboy of the Western World, Peer Gynt, Romeo and Juliet* (RNT); *Protestants* (Traverse/ Soho); *Dealer's Choice, My Night With Reg* (Birmingham Rep); *The Merchant of Venice* (RSC); *Pentecost* (Donmar/ Kennedy Centre, Washington); *Drink, Dance, Laugh, Lie* (Bush Theatre); *In A Little World Of Our Own* (Donmar); *The Deep Blue Sea* (Royal Exchange); *Red Roses And Petrol, Lady Windermere's Fan, The Ash Fire* (Tricycle); *Howling Moon Silent Sons, The Plough and the Stars, The Silver Tassie, Aristrocrats* (Abbey Theatre); *Spokesong, Shiver* (Rough Magic). **Television** includes *Inspector Lynley* series IV & V, Stephen Poliakoff's new film *Friends and Crocodiles, Murder City, Rebel Heart, Father Ted, The Informant, The Governor, Nighthawks*. **Film** includes *Though the Sky Falls, Nora, Ordinary Decent Criminal, The General, The American, The Matchmaker, Moll Flanders, On the Edge, Saving Private Ryan, Spin the Bottle*.

SUSAN LYNCH

Previous appearances at the **Royal Court** include *Ashes and Sand* and *Berlin Bertie*. Other **theatre** includes *The Night Season*, *Pericles* and *Le Cid* (National Theatre); *Mnemonic* (Complicite); *The Storm* (Almeida); *Miss Julie* (Young Vic); *The Clearing* (Bush/ National Theatre); *Tube*, *Richard II* (Royal Exchange, Manchester); *The Honey Spike*, *The Last Ones* (Abbey Theatre, Dublin); *Lulu* (Cambridge Theatre Company). **Television** includes *Soundproof*, *10 Commandments*, *Bodies*, *Any Time Now*, *Sweet Revenge*, *Amongst Women*, *Kings in Grass Castles*, *Ivanhoe*, *A Royal Scandal*, *Truth or Dare*, *The Perfect Match*, *Dangerous Lady*, *Cracker*, *As You Like It*. **Film** includes *Someone Else*, *Mickeybo and Me*, *Enduring Love*, *Duane Hopwood*, *Casa De Los Babys*, *16 Years of Alcohol*, *Happy Now*, *From Hell*, *Beautiful Creatures*, *Nora*, *Jedermanns Fest*, *Deceit*, *Waking Ned*, *Downtime*, *Secret of Roan Inish*.

AOIFE McMAHON

Aoife is from County Clare and attended the Royal Academy of Dramatic Art in London. **Theatre** includes Lady Macbeth in *Macbeth* (Derby Playhouse); *Gates of Gold* (Finborough Arms); Beauty in *Beauty and the Beast* (RSC); *Scenes from the Big Picture* (National Theatre); *Dancing at Lughnasa* (Greenwich Theatre/Watermill, Newbury); *Pains of Youth* (National Theatre Studio); *Andorra* (Young Vic); *The Playboy of the Western World* (Liverpool Playhouse); *Oriana* (Kabosh); *Deirdre* (Armagh Rhymers Theatre). **Television** and **film** work includes *My Dad's the Prime Minister*, *The Clinic*, *Steel River Blues*, *Holy Cross* for BBC Films. She won the 2002 Gemini Award (Canadian Bafta) for Best Actress for her role in *Random Passage*. **Radio** includes *Hippomania* and *Baldi* (BBC).

GEMMA REEVES

Theatre includes *The Drunkard* (Olympia Theatre, Dublin and tour); *The Cherry Orchard* (Abbey Theatre); *Pygmalion* (Gate Theatre); *The Playboy of the Western World* (Perth Arts Festival); *Riders to the Sea*, *The Playboy of The Western World* and *Deirdre of the Sorrows* – all part of the DruidSynge Cycle (Town Hall, Galway, Olympia Theatre, Dublin, and Edinburgh Festival 2005). **Television** includes *Malice Aforethought* and *Pride and Joy*.

MOSSIE SMITH

Previous appearances at the **Royal Court** include *Road, Shirley, The Recruiting Officer, Our Country's Good* and *Three Birds Alighting on a Field*. Other **theatre** includes *Longitude* (Greenwich Theatre); *Getting to the Foot of the Mountain* (Birmingham Rep); *Howard Katz* and *Wild Oats* (National Theatre); *Sex Please, We're Italian* and *The Crucible* (Young Vic); *Blithe Spirit* (Bromley); *Babes in the Wood* (Salisbury); *See How They Run* (Canterbury); and *Oh Dear Purcell!* (Stationers' Hall). **Television** includes regular appearances as Aunt Megan in *Hearts of Gold* and Petula Belcher in *The Riff-Raff Element*. Other appearances include *2000 Streets Under the Sky, In Deep, The Bill, Midsomer Murders, Undercover Heart, Goodnight Mr Tom, Tom Jones, Rough Justice, French and Saunders, Harry Enfield and Chums, The Widowing of Mrs Holroyd, Absolutely Fabulous, Casualty, Prime Suspect I* and *IV, Heroes and Villains, Mr Wakefield's Crusade, Queen of the East, Come Home Charlie and Face Them, A Very Peculiar Practice, Road, Putting on the Ritz, Rat in the Skull, South of the Border, Wuffer, Reith, Give us a Break, Number 10, I'm a Stranger Here Myself, The Woman in White* and *Tiny Revolutions*. **Film** includes *Two Men Went To War, House, Breathtaking, Janice Beard 45 wpm, The Girl with Brains in her Feet, Up the Valley, Second Best* and *Memoirs of a Survivor*. **Radio** includes *Desmond Olivier Dingle's Complete Life and Works of William Shakespeare*.

EWAN STEWART

Previous appearances at the **Royal Court** include *At the Table/Almost Nothing, Sacred Heart, Trade, Bluebird, Thyestes, Live Like Pigs, Flying Blind,* and *Road* (Royal Court and national tour). Other **theatre** includes *The Pillowman* (National Theatre tour); *Green Field, The Orphans Comedy, Lucy's Play* (Traverse Theatre); *Sisters, Brothers* (The Gate); *The Duchess of Malfi* (Bristol Old Vic); *A Working Woman* (West Yorkshire Playhouse); *Phoenix* (Bush Theatre); *Racing Demon, The Murderer, Major Barbara, Sergeant Musgrave's Dance, A Month in the Country, In the Blue* and *As I Lay Dying* (National Theatre); *When We Were Women* (National Theatre Studio); *Weights and Measures* (National Theatre Workshop); *A Midsummer Night's Dream* (Scottish Opera); season at Durham Theatre. **Television** includes *Malice Aforethought, Dirty War, POW, Real Men, Touch And Go, Looking After Jo Jo, Nervous Energy, A Mug's Game, Down Among The Big Boys, Spender, The Bill, The Advocates, Eurocops III – Pushed, Boon, Dream Baby, Only Fools And Horses, Biting The Hand, Radical Chambers, The Shutter Falls, Flight To Berlin, Good And Bad At Games, A Woman Calling, Anthony And Cleopatra, Ill Fares The Land, Green Street Revisisted, Quiet Days Of Mrs Stafford, The Professionals, Mackenzie, Barriers, Rain On The Roof, Shadows On Our Skin, The Camerons*. **Film** included *Alpha Male, Young Adam, One Last Chance, Conspiracy, The Last Great Wilderness, Untitled Irish Comedy, Big Brass Ring, Titanic, Stella Does Tricks, Rob Roy, Kafka, The Cook The Thief His Wife And Her Lover, Resurrected, Paradise Postponed, Not Quite Jerusalem, Remembrance, Who Dares Wins, All Quiet On The Western Front*.

STELLA FEEHILY
(Writer)

Stella Feehily's debut play, *Duck*, was produced by Out of Joint and the Royal Court. She has worked as an actress for ten years. *O go my Man* is her second full-length play.

MAX STAFFORD-CLARK
(Director)

Founded Joint Stock Theatre Group in 1974 following his Artistic Directorship of the Traverse Theatre, Edinburgh. From 1979 to 1993 he was Artistic Director of the Royal Court. In 1993 he founded Out of Joint. His work as a director has overwhelmingly been with new writing and he has commissioned and directed first productions by many of the country's leading writers.

ES DEVLIN
(Set Designer)

Es trained first in music, English literature and fine art before attending the Motley course in Stage Design. She has been designing for stage since 1996. Previous designs for Out of Joint include *Macbeth*, *Rita, Sue and Bob Too/A State Affair* (with Soho) and *Hinterland* (with RNT). For the Royal Court: *Dumb Show*, *Credible Witness* and *Yard Gal*. Es's most recent designs include US rapper Kanye West's American tour and *All the Ordinary Angels* for Manchester Royal Exchange, nominated for MEN Best Design 2005. Other theatre includes *Hecuba*, *Dog in the Manger*, *Antony and Cleopatra*, *Henry IV* and *The Prisoner's Dilemma* (RSC); *Betrayal* (National Theatre); *Five Gold Rings* (Almeida); *Flag Burning* with Jake and Dinos Chapman and *Wire* (Barbican); *A Day in*

the Death of Joe Egg (Comedy Theatre/Broadway); *Arabian Night* (ATC); *Piano* (TPT Tokyo); *Airsick*, *Love and Understanding*, *Howie the Rookie* (Bush Theatre, winner TMA Best Design 1998); *The Death of Cool* (Hampstead Theatre); *Hamlet* (Young Vic); *Perapalas* (Gate); *Meat* (Plymouth Theatre Royal, nominated TMA Best Design 2000); *Closer to Heaven*, the Pet Shop Boys Musical (Arts Theatre); *Edward II* (Bolton Octagon, winner Linbury Prize for Stage Designer 1996). Designs for dance include *Essence* (ROH Linbury); *Four Scenes* and *God's Plenty* (Rambert); *A Streetcar Named Desire* (Northern Ballet Theatre) and *I Remember Red* (Cullberg Ballet Sweden). Production Designs for film are *Brilliant!*, *Snow on Saturday* and *Victoria Station*. Opera includes *Orphee* (ROH Linbury); *Macbeth* (Klangbogen Festival Vienna); *Powder Her Face* (Ystad Festival, Sweden); *Fidelio* (English Touring Opera); *Hansel and Gretel* (Scottish Opera Go Round). Es is currently working on *A Midsummer Night's Dream* (Hamburg State Opera), *Don Giovanni /Flammen* (Theater an der Wien, Vienna), *La Clemenza di Tito* (Opera del Liceo Barcelona) and *Qaddafi*, in collaboration with Asian Dub Foundation for ENO. View Es's work at www.esdevlin.com

EMMA WILLIAMS
(Costume Designer)

Emma has designed costumes extensively within the fields of film, theatre and television. She works regularly with the Royal Shakespeare Company (including most recently the

Spanish Golden Age and Tragedies Seasons and *The Canterbury Tales*); National Theatre, Out of Joint and on numerous productions in the West End. She has also worked at Chichester Festival Theatre, Oxford Stage Company, English Touring Theatre and the Royal Opera House, Covent Garden. Her film credits include *Chunky Monkey, Nouvelle France, Cornejo en la Luna* and *Fingers Crossed*. Television credits include Michael Wood's series *Myths & Legends* and *Elmina's Kitchen* for BBC3.

JOHANNA TOWN
(Lighting Designer)

Other Out of Joint and Royal Court co-productions include: *Talking to Terrorists, Duck; Shopping & Fucking* (also West End/New York) and *The Steward of Christendom* (also New York). Also for Out of Joint: *Macbeth; The Permanent Way* (also RNT/Australia); *She Stoops to Conquer, A Laughing Matter* (also RNT); *Feelgood* (also Hampstead/West End); *Our Lady of Sligo* (also RNT/New York). Other New York theatre includes *Guantanamo* (& Tricycle/West End); *Rose* (& RNT) and *Arabian Nights* and other West End productions include *Little Malcolm & His Struggle Against the Eunuchs* (& Hampstead); *Top Girls, Via Dolorosa* and *Beautiful Thing*. She has been Head of Lighting at the Royal Court since 1990 where recent lighting designs include: *My Name is Rachel Corrie, Way to Heaven, A Girl in a Car with a Man, Under the Whaleback, Plasticine, Mr Kolpert* and *The Kitchen* and her other recent freelance lighting designs include *All the Ordinary Angels*, *Six Degrees of Separation*, *Ghosts*, *Misfits*, *Richard II* and *The Lodger* (Royal Exchange); *Dead Funny* (West Yorkshire Playhouse); *East Coast Chicken Supper* (Traverse, winner of Fringe First); *A Brief History of Helen of Troy* (ATC); *Someone Who'll Watch Over Me* (Northampton); *How Love Is Spelt* (Bush); *I.D.* (Almeida/BBC3); *Badnuff* (Soho); *The Dumb Waiter* (Oxford) and *Popcorn* (Liverpool Playhouse).

GARETH FRY
(Sound Designer)

Gareth worked with Out of Joint on *Talking to Terrorists* (with the Royal Court) and *Macbeth*. He trained at the Central School of Speech and Drama in theatre design. His work as a sound designer and occasionally as a composer includes: For Complicite: *Strange Poetry* (with the LA Philharmonic Orchestra), *Noise of Time* (with the Emerson String Quartet), *Mnemonic* (associate), *Genoa 01*. For the National Theatre, UK: *Theatre of Blood*, *Fix Up*, *Iphigenia at Aulis*, *The Three Sisters*, *Ivanov*, *The Oresteia*. For the Royal Court: *Harvest*, *Forty Winks*, *Under the Whaleback*, *Night Songs*, *Face to the Wall*, *Redundant*, *Mountain Language*, *Ashes to Ashes*, *The Country*. Other work includes: *Almost Blue* (Riverside Studios, Associate Director); *Phaedra's Love* (Bristol Old Vic/Barbican); *Astronaut* (Theatre O); *The Bull*, *Giselle* (Fabulous Beast); *Zero Degrees and Drifting* (Unlimited Theatre); *Living Costs* (DV8 at Tate Modern); *Red Night* (Finborough Theatre); *The Watery Part of the World* (BAC); *By the Bog of Cats* (Wyndhams Theatre); *Blithe Spirit* (Savoy Theatre);

Chimps (Liverpool Playhouse); *Time and Space* (Living Dance Studio, Beijing); *Shape of Metal* (Abbey, Dublin); *World Music*, *The Dark* (Donmar Warehouse); *A Midsummer Night's Dream* (Regent's Park Open Air Theatre); *Eccentricities of a Nightingale* (Gate, Dublin); *The Found Man*, *Mr. Placebo* (Traverse); *Forbidden Broadway* (Albery); *Holy Mothers* (New Ambassadors); *The Scarlett Letter*, *The Accrington Pals* (Chichester); *Wexford Trilogy* (OSC); *Play to Win* (Yellow Earth). He also designs the music and sound systems for Somerset House's ice rink. More info at www.garethfry.co.uk

FELIX CROSS
(Composer)

Felix worked with Out of Joint on *Talking to Terrorists* (with the Royal Court) and *Macbeth*. He is Artistic Director of NITRO where he has worked on *High Heel Parrotfish*, *Slamdunk*, *ICED*, *Passports to the Promised Land*, *Tricksters*, *Payback*, *Up Against The Wall*. He has produced four years of the NITRObeat festival, and *A NITRO At The Opera* in partnership with the Royal Opera House. Other work includes: *Blues For Railton*, *Glory!*; *Mass Carib*; *Integration Octet* (for string quartet and steel pan quartet); *Jekyll & Hyde* and *The Bottle Imp*. He regularly composes for radio dramas and has also written music for over fifty stage plays including the entire canon of Agatha Christie's plays. He directed *The Panbeaters* for Greenwich Theatre and has also directed plays for Radio 4.

NAOMI JONES
(Assistant Director)

Directing credits include *Amadeus* (Edinburgh Fringe), *Three Sisters* (Contact Theatre), *Blue Remembered Hills* (Courtyard Theatre) and *Bloody Poetry* (Brockley Jack Theatre). For Out of Joint, Naomi has worked on *Talking to Terrorists*, *Macbeth*, *The Permanent Way* and *Duck* and was Associate Director on *Sisters, Such Devoted Sisters*. She recently directed a rehearsed reading of *Reception* (Out of Joint/Soho).

GRAHAM COWLEY
(Producer)

Out of Joint's Producer since 1998. His long collaboration with Max Stafford-Clark began as Joint Stock Theatre Group's first General Manager for seven years in the 1970s. He was General Manager of the Royal Court for eight years, and on their behalf transferred a string of hit plays to the West End. His career has spanned the full range of theatre production, from small fringe companies to major West End shows and large scale commercial tours. Outside Out of Joint, he has most recently produced the notorious *Harry and Me* at the Warehouse Theatre, his own translation of *End of Story* at the Chelsea Theatre and the fiercely anti-war *Forgotten Voices from the Great War* series, starting with a season at the Pleasance London and followed by *What the Women Did* at Southwark Playhouse and most recently *Red Night* at the Finborough Theatre in November 2005.

out of joint

Out of Joint is a national and international touring theatre company dedicated to the production of new writing. Under the direction of Max Stafford-Clark the company has premiered plays from leading writers including David Hare, Caryl Churchill, Mark Ravenhill, Sebastian Barry and Timberlake Wertenbaker, as well as first-time writers such as Simon Bennett and Stella Feehily, whose *Duck* for Out of Joint was 2003's hit in Edinburgh, London and Dublin.

'You expect something special from the touring company Out of Joint ...
here's to their next ten years' **The Times 2004**

Touring all over the UK, Out of Joint frequently performs at and co-produces with key venues including the Royal Court, the National Theatre, Hampstead Theatre, the Liverpool Everyman & Playhouse, Soho Theatre and the Young Vic. By co-producing its work the company is able to maintain an on-going repertoire as well as premiering two new plays a year. Out of Joint is classed as one of the British Council's 'flagship' touring companies, and has performed in six continents – most recently during the world tour of its Africa-inspired *Macbeth* which played in the United States, Mexico, the Czech Republic, the Netherlands and Nigeria. Back home, Out of Joint pursues an extensive education programme, with workshops in schools, universities and colleges.

'Max Stafford-Clark's excellent Out of Joint company'
The Independent 2004

Out of Joint's challenging and high profile work has gained the company an international reputation and awards including the prestigious Prudential Award for Theatre. With a continuing commitment from Arts Council England, Out of Joint continues to commission, develop and produce new writing of the highest calibre. Out of Joint's most recent production was *Talking to Terrorists* by Robin Soans, based on real-life interviews conducted by the writer and the company.

'Out of Joint is out of this world' **Boston Globe 2005**

out of joint

OjO education work
Out of Joint offers a diverse programme of workshops and discussions for groups coming to see our performances. For full details of our education programme, resource packs or *Our Country's Good* workshops, contact Max or Tasha at Out of Joint.

Out of Joint
Post:	7 Thane Works, Thane Villas, London N7 7NU
Tel:	020 7609 0207
Fax:	020 7609 0203
Email:	ojo@outofjoint.co.uk
Website:	www.outofjoint.co.uk

Out of Joint is grateful to the following for their support over the years:
Arts Council England, The Foundation for Sport and the Arts, The Baring Foundation, The Paul Hamlyn Foundation, The Olivier Foundation, The Peggy Ramsay Foundation, The John S Cohen Foundation, The David Cohen Charitable Trust, The National Lottery through the Arts Council of England, The Prudential Awards, Stephen Evans, Karl Sydow, Harold Stokes and Friends of Theatre, John Lewis Partnership, Royal Victoria Hall Foundation

ARTS COUNCIL ENGLAND

Out of Joint is a registered charity 1033059

KEEP IN TOUCH
For information on our shows, tour details and offers, call us on 0207 609 0207, email ojo@outofjoint.co.uk or send your contact details to Out of Joint, 7 Thane Works, Thane Villas, London N7 7NU, letting us know whether you'd like to receive information by post or email.

out of joint

Past productions

2005
Talking to Terrorists by Robin Soans

2004
Macbeth by William Shakespeare

2003
The Permanent Way by David Hare
Duck by Stella Feehily

2002
A Laughing Matter by April De Angelis
    & *She Stoops to Conquer* by Oliver Goldsmith
Hinterland by Sebastian Barry

2001
Sliding with Suzanne by Judy Upton
Feelgood by Alistair Beaton

2000
Rita, Sue and Bob Too by Andrea Dunbar
    & *A State Affair* by Robin Soans

1999
Some Explicit Polaroids by Mark Ravenhill
Drummers by Simon Bennett

1998
Our Country's Good by Timberlake Wertenbaker
Our Lady of Sligo by Sebastian Barry

1997
Blue Heart by Caryl Churchill
The Positive Hour by April De Angelis

1996
Shopping and Fucking by Mark Ravenhill

1995
The Steward of Christendom by Sebastian Barry
Three Sisters by Anton Chekhov
    & *The Break of Day* by Timberlake Wertenbaker

1994
The Man of Mode by George Etherege
    & *The Libertine* by Stephen Jeffreys
The Queen and I by Sue Townsend
    & *Road* by Jim Cartwright

Top: Blue Heart, Out of Joint/Royal Court, 1997 (photo Donald Cooper). Middle: Macbeth, Out of Joint, 2004 (photo John Haynes). Bottom: Shopping and Fucking, Out of Joint/Royal Court, 1996 (photo John Haynes).

THE ENGLISH STAGE COMPANY AT THE ROYAL COURT

The English Stage Company at the Royal Court opened in 1956 as a subsidised theatre producing new British plays, international plays and some classical revivals.

The first artistic director George Devine aimed to create a writers' theatre, 'a place where the dramatist is acknowledged as the fundamental creative force in the theatre and where the play is more important than the actors, the director, the designer'. The urgent need was to find a contemporary style in which the play, the acting, direction and design are all combined. He believed that 'the battle will be a long one to continue to create the right conditions for writers to work in'.

Devine aimed to discover 'hard-hitting, uncompromising writers whose plays are stimulating, provocative and exciting'. The Royal Court production of John Osborne's Look Back in Anger in May 1956 is now seen as the decisive starting point of modern British drama and the policy created a new generation of British playwrights. The first wave included John Osborne, Arnold Wesker, John Arden, Ann Jellicoe, N F Simpson and Edward Bond. Early seasons included new international plays by Bertolt Brecht, Eugène Ionesco, Samuel Beckett, Jean-Paul Sartre and Marguerite Duras.

The theatre started with the 400-seat proscenium arch Theatre Downstairs, and in 1969 opened a second theatre, the 60-seat studio Theatre Upstairs. Some productions transfer to the West End, such as Terry Johnson's Hitchcock Blonde, Caryl Churchill's Far Away and Conor McPherson's The Weir. Recent touring productions include Sarah Kane's 4.48 Psychosis (US tour) and Ché Walker's Flesh Wound (Galway Arts Festival). The Royal Court also co-produces plays which transfer to the West End or tour internationally, such as Conor McPherson's Shining City (with Gate Theatre, Dublin), Sebastian Barry's The Steward of Christendom and Mark Ravenhill's Shopping and Fucking (with Out of Joint), Martin McDonagh's The Beauty Queen Of Leenane (with Druid), Ayub Khan Din's East is East (with Tamasha).

Since 1994 the Royal Court's artistic policy has again been vigorously directed to finding and producing a new generation of playwrights. The writers include Joe Penhall, Rebecca Prichard, Michael Wynne, Nick Grosso, Judy Upton, Meredith Oakes, Sarah Kane, Anthony Neilson, Judith Johnson, James Stock, Jez Butterworth, Marina Carr, Phyllis Nagy, Simon Block, Martin

photo: Andy Chopping

McDonagh, Mark Ravenhill, Ayub Khan Din, Tamantha Hammerschlag, Jess Walters, Ché Walker, Conor McPherson, Simon Stephens, Richard Bean, Roy Williams, Gary Mitchell, Mick Mahoney, Rebecca Gilman, Christopher Shinn, Kia Corthron, David Gieselmann, Marius von Mayenburg, David Eldridge, Leo Butler, Zinnie Harris, Grae Cleugh, Roland Schimmelpfennig, Chloe Moss, DeObia Oparei, Enda Walsh, Vassily Sigarev, the Presnyakov Brothers, Marcos Barbosa, Lucy Prebble, John Donnelly, Clare Pollard, Robin French, Elyzabeth Gregory Wilder, Rob Evans, Laura Wade and Debbie Tucker Green. This expanded programme of new plays has been made possible through the support of A.S.K. Theater Projects and the Skirball Foundation, The Jerwood Charity, the American Friends of the Royal Court Theatre and (in 1994/5 and 1999) in association with the National Theatre Studio.

In recent years there have been record-breaking productions at the box office, with capacity houses for Joe Penhall's Dumb Show, Conor McPherson's Shining City, Roy Williams' Fallout and Terry Johnson's Hitchcock Blonde.

The refurbished theatre in Sloane Square opened in February 2000, with a policy still inspired by the first artistic director George Devine. The Royal Court is an international theatre for new plays and new playwrights, and the work shapes contemporary drama in Britain and overseas.

PROGRAMME SUPPORTERS

The Royal Court (English Stage Company Ltd) receives its principal funding from Arts Council England, London. It is also supported financially by a wide range of private companies, charitable and public bodies, and earns the remainder of its income from the box office and its own trading activities.

The Genesis Foundation supports the Royal Court's work with International Playwrights.

The Jerwood Charity supports new plays by new playwrights through the Jerwood New Playwrights series.

The Skirball Foundation funds a Playwrights' Programme at the theatre. The Artistic Director's Chair is supported by a lead grant from The Peter Jay Sharp Foundation, contributing to the activities of the Artistic Director's office. Bloomberg Mondays, the Royal Court's reduced price ticket scheme, is supported by Bloomberg. Over the past nine years the BBC has supported the Gerald Chapman Fund for directors.

ROYAL COURT
DEVELOPMENT BOARD
Tamara Ingram (Chair)
Jonathan Cameron
(Vice Chair)
Timothy Burrill
Anthony Burton
Jonathan Caplan QC
Sindy Caplan
Gavin Casey FCA
Mark Crowdy
Cas Donald
Joseph Fiennes
Amanda Foreman
Joyce Hytner OBE
Gavin Neath
Michael Potter
Kadee Robbins
Mark Robinson
William Russell
Sue Stapely
James L Tanner
Will Turner

PUBLIC FUNDING
Arts Council England, London
British Council
London Challenge
Royal Borough of Kensington & Chelsea

TRUSTS AND
FOUNDATIONS
The ADAPT Trust
American Friends of the Royal Court Theatre
Gerald Chapman Fund
Columbia Foundation
Cowley Charitable Trust
The Dorset Foundation
The Ronald Duncan Literary Foundation
The Foundation for Sport and the Arts
The Foyle Foundation
Francis Finlay Foundation
The Garfield Weston Foundation
Genesis Foundation
Jerwood Charity
Lynn Foundation
John Lyon's Charity

The Magowan Family Foundation
The Rayne Foundation
Rose Foundation
The Royal Victoria Hall Foundation
The Peter Jay Sharp Foundation
Skirball Foundation
The Bruce Wake Charitable Trust
Michael J Zamkow & Sue E Berman Charitable Trust

50TH ANNIVERSARY
PROGRAMME SPONSOR
Coutts & Co

CORPORATE
BENEFACTORS
Insinger De Beaufort
Merrill Lynch

SPONSORS
Arts & Business New Partners
BBC
Bloomberg
Cadogan Hotel
Doughty Street Chamber
John Malkovich/Uncle Kimono
Simons Muirhead & Burton

BUSINESS AND MEDIA
MEMBERS
Aviva plc
Bloomsbury
Columbia Tristar Films (UK)
The Henley Centre
Peter Jones
Lazard
Slaughter and May

PRODUCTION
SYNDICATE
Anonymous
Ms Kay Ellen Consolver
Mrs Philip Donald
Peter & Edna Goldstein

Richard & Robin Landsberger
Kadee Robbins
William & Hilary Russell
Kay Hartenstein Saatchi
Jon & NoraLee Sedmak
Ian & Carol Sellars
James & Victoria Tanner

INDIVIDUAL MEMBERS
Patrons
Anonymous
Dr Bettina Bahlsen
Katie Bradford
Marcus J Burton & Dr M F Ozbilgin
Mr & Mrs Philip Donald
Celeste Fenichel
Tom & Simone Fenton
Daniel & Joanna Friel
Lady Grabiner
Charles & Elizabeth Handy
Jack & Linda Keenan
Pawel & Sarah Kisielewski
Duncan Matthews QC
Ian & Carol Sellars
Jan & Michael Topham
Richard Wilson OBE

Benefactors
Anonymous
Martha Allfrey
Amanda Attard-Manché
Varian Ayers & Gary Knisely
John & Anoushka Ayton
Mr & Mrs Gavin Casey
Sindy & Jonathan Caplan
Jeremy Conway & Nicola Van Gelder
Robyn Durie
Joachim Fleury
Beverley Gee
Sue and Don Guiney
Tamara Ingram
David Juxon
David Kaskell & Christopher Teano
Peter & Maria Kellner
Deborah & Stephen Marquardt
Barbara Minto

Mr & Mrs Richard Pilosof
Anthony Simpson
Brian D Smith
Sue Stapeley
Sir Robert & Lady Wilson
Nick Wheeler
Wendy Wolstonecraft
Sir Mark & Lady Wrightson

Associates
Act IV
Anonymous
Jeffrey Archer
Brian Boylan
Alan Brodie
Ossi & Paul Burger
Mrs Helena Butler
Lady Cazalet
Carole & Neville Conrad
Margaret Cowper
Andrew Cryer
Linda & Ronald F. Daitz
Zoë Dominic
Kim Dunn
Charlotte & Nick Fraser
Gillian Frumkin
Sara Galbraith
Jacqueline & Jonathan Gestetner
Vivien Goodwin
P. Hobbs - LTRC
David & Suzie Hyman
Mrs Ellen Josefowitz
Mr & Mrs Tarek Kassem
Carole A. Leng
Colette & Peter Levy
Mr Watcyn Lewis
David Marks
Nicola McFarland
Gavin & Ann Neath
Janet & Michael Orr
Pauline Pinder
William Poeton CBE & Barbara Poeton
Jan & Michael Potter
Jeremy Priestley
Beverley Rider
John Ritchie
Lois Sieff OBE
Gail Steele
Will Turner
Anthony Wigram

JERWOOD
NEW PLAYWRIGHTS

Since 1994 Jerwood New Playwrights has contributed to 47 new plays at the Royal Court including Joe Penhall's SOME VOICES, Mark Ravenhill's SHOPPING AND FUCKING (co-production with Out of Joint), Ayub Khan Din's EAST IS EAST (co-production with Tamasha), Martin McDonagh's THE BEAUTY QUEEN OF LEENANE (co-production with Druid Theatre Company), Conor McPherson's THE WEIR, Nick Grosso's REAL CLASSY AFFAIR, Sarah Kane's 4.48 PSYCHOSIS, Gary Mitchell's THE FORCE OF CHANGE, David Eldridge's UNDER THE BLUE SKY, David Harrower's PRESENCE, Simon Stephens' HERONS, Roy Williams' CLUBLAND, Leo Butler's REDUNDANT, Michael Wynne's THE PEOPLE ARE FRIENDLY, David Greig's OUTLYING ISLANDS, Zinnie Harris' NIGHTINGALE AND CHASE, Grae Cleugh's FUCKING GAMES, Rona Munro's IRON, Richard Bean's UNDER THE WHALEBACK, Ché Walker's FLESH WOUND, Roy Williams' FALLOUT, Mick Mahoney's FOOD CHAIN, Ayub Khan Din's NOTES ON FALLING LEAVES, Leo Butler's LUCKY DOG, Simon Stephens' COUNTRY MUSIC, Laura Wade's BREATHING CORPSES, Debbie Tucker Green's STONING MARY, David Eldridge's INCOMPLETE AND RANDOM ACTS OF KINDNESS, and Gregory Burke's ON TOUR.

In 2006, Jerwood New Playwrights are supporting O GO MY MAN by Stella Feehily, MOTORTOWN by Simon Stephens, and RAINBOW KISS by Simon Farquhar.

The Jerwood Charitable Foundation is a registered charity dedicated to imaginative and responsible funding of the arts and other areas of human endeavour and excellence.

Leo Butler's LUCKY DOG
(photo: Ivan Kyncl)

David Eldridge's INCOMPLETE AND RANDOM
ACTS OF KINDNESS
(photo: Keith Pattison)

FOR THE ROYAL COURT

Acknowledgements

I would like to thank Ruth Little for reading drafts of the script and her invaluable advice. Thanks to Graham Whybrow and Ian Rickson for guidance, Paul Cunningham and Jon Snow for expertise, Jürgen Teller, Sadie and Ed for an extraordinary photo shoot, the cast – Denise Gough, Sam Graham, Paul Hickey, Susan Lynch, Aoife McMahon, Gemma Reeves, Mossie Smith and Ewan Stewart for constant scrutiny and support. Finally, thanks to Max Stafford-Clark who has been influential in the play's structure and all stages of its development.

Theatre is truly a collaborative art and without the help of all these colleagues I would not have written this play as it stands.

S.F.
December 2005

O GO MY MAN

Stella Feehily

For Karen

Characters

NEIL, *forty-five*
SARAH, *thirties*
IAN, *forty*
ELSA, *twenties*
ZOË, *thirties*
MAGGIE, *fifteen*
ALICE,
    a waitress, a chambermaid, a bag lady, a patient, a cleaner
The QUEEN OF HEARTS
A DIRECTOR
JIM, *a news editor*
FREDDY, *a floor manager*
REG, *a P.A.*
An EX-SERGEANT
The WHITE RABBIT

/ indicates overlapping dialogue.

This text went to press before the end of rehearsals so may differ slightly from the play as performed.

Scene One

Sudan. NEIL *is talking on a satellite phone.*

NEIL. We did it. We got it.

Thought it wasn't going to happen but we pushed and we pushed.

The camps, the refugees, the burnt villages, na na na na.

It was OK OK what we had – but we were desperate to make the extra –

The money shot.

Tanya is going mental – stranded in Nyala – but I was fucked if I was rushing back to focus on IDPs again. We were following the Janjaweed.

There's going to be trouble tomorrow not least that it's taken a UN escort to get us to El Fasher – more anon.

Anyway, can't set up the generator. Can't go outside. Question of safety.

We'll fly to Khartoum first thing. Send the report up the line on our own satellite.

I'm back Wednesday morning. I just want to tell you – I just want to tell you – I am so fucking pumped.

It's midnight and I want to tell you everything.

Scene Two

Morning. Sunlight.

IAN *is looking out his bedroom window. He lines up to take a photograph.*

He is shirtless and wearing jeans.

He takes a picture as SARAH *enters. She is in her underwear.*

SARAH. There's a law against that.

SARAH *rifles through some articles of clothing.*

IAN. I'm making art.

SARAH. Who are you photographing?

IAN. You. I'm getting your reflection in the glass.

You look like a ghost.

Wandering about my room.

SARAH. Your room, is it?

She pulls out a T-shirt.

IAN. Ours, I meant ours.

Don't use that as a way to start an argument.

SARAH. Why would I do that?

IAN. It's what you do.

You going out?

SARAH. Yes.

She puts it back.

IAN. Pleasure? Work?

SARAH. Audition for a breakfast cereal. I told you.

I need to look 'Young Mum'. Suggestions?

IAN. A stained T-shirt and a depressed look.

Though you have the latter.

She picks up another item of clothing.

He takes a photograph.

SARAH. Ho ho – Ian.

IAN. I'm thinking authenticity.

SARAH. I don't want authenticity – And neither do they.

She discards it.

Look at that. (*Holding out her hand.*)

IAN. What? I see nothing.

SARAH. A tremor. I'm nervous already.

IAN. About what?

She tries on a dress.

SARAH. I would like the director to say – you could shift 'All-Brown' in vast quantities. I need someone to believe in me.

IAN. I believe in you.

She takes it off and throws it down.

SARAH. Thanks. Anyway, I'm not going to get it.

IAN. Bollocks – you don't know.

She hunts out some fishnets and socks – a quirky piece of clothing.

SARAH. Ian. Last week I auditioned for the part of a thirty-something.

I was told I was too old. It's fucked.

I may even be too old for 'Young Mum'.

IAN. I thought you said your agent had you up for something?

SARAH. *Alice in Wonderland.*

IAN. You can't be too old if *Wonderland* wants you.

SARAH. Yes – however, it's *Wonderland* not *Woyzeck*. I shall have difficulty getting up on that horse called Dignity. (*She pulls on a pair of long socks.*)

I should have gone into psychiatry like I wanted to. Have you seen my boots?

IAN. Bathroom.

SARAH *exits.*

I nearly broke my neck on them.

SARAH. Thanks.

She re-enters carrying the boots.

You know what, Ian?

She sits and pulls on her boots.

IAN. What?

SARAH. For years I've felt as if I was on the cusp of something and this morning I realised what it was.

IAN. What?

SARAH. Middle age.

She picks up a T-shirt.

IAN. Wait till you're forty then talk to me about middle age.

SARAH. But you look younger – why?

IAN. Why?

SARAH. You're not ambitious so you're not bitter.

IAN. I am fucking bitter. I'm just ageing better than you are.

SARAH. So why don't you do something?

Get your stuff out there.

IAN. You haven't a clue, Sarah.

SARAH *potters about. All the while,* IAN *watches.*

He takes a photograph.

SARAH. I don't want to be photographed in my underwear.

IAN. People like looking at you. OK. I like looking at you.

What do you think of that?

SARAH. What do I think?

He moves towards her.

SARAH *avoids him and moves away.*

One of us has got to make some money.

If 'All-Brown' want me to defecate on a plate – I'll do it.

IAN. I've got a job this morning.

SARAH. Why didn't you say?

Will you pay the car tax? It's three months out of date.

IAN. Ask me what it is.

SARAH. What is it?

She exits to bathroom.

IAN. I'm shooting Michael Farrell.

SARAH. Jesus. Does the world need another celebrity chef?

SARAH re-enters brushing her teeth.

IAN. But he's hot, yeah?

SARAH. A marketing wet dream. (*She exits to spit.*) Plastered over every celebrity rag.

(*Shouts from off.*) His wife is the former head of a PR company. Gave it up to have babies.

She re-enters.

He photographs her. She picks up a skirt.

IAN. How do you know this shit?

SARAH. It's called column inches.

What's your involvement?

She puts the skirt on.

IAN. He's supporting a Human Rights event.

SARAH. Of course he is.

Because he can throw a bit of parmesan over asparagus he's a diplomat.

So you won't be paying the car tax?

IAN. Probably not.

Do you still love me?

SARAH. What?

IAN. A simple yes or no will do.

She picks up a pair of jeans and examines them.

SARAH. I love you.

She discards the jeans.

IAN. I've been feeling bad.

SARAH. Why?

IAN. Can you tell me?

SARAH. I can't tell you why you're feeling bad.

IAN. We're OK, aren't we? How are we?

She walks towards a mirror and teases out her hair.

SARAH. Do you feel the need to take our temperature today?

IAN. Sarah – let's not say no to one another any more.

I can't bear it.

SARAH. I don't say 'no' all the time.

IAN. It's been five months.

SARAH. God. Well. There you go.

IAN. There you go, what?

I want to fuck you.

I want to love you.

I want to piss in your mouth.

SARAH. Jesus, Ian . . .

Can't you have a wank like everyone else?

SARAH's mobile phone rings.

She takes it out of her bag – looks at the number and knocks it off.

He holds the camera up.

No more pictures.

IAN. Who was that?

SARAH. One of the girls. I don't have time.

He takes a photograph.

IAN. Who? Karen?

SARAH. Yeah.

IAN. Don't you fancy me any more?

SARAH. OK. I'll give you a quick hand job.

IAN. You make it sound like emptying the bin.

SARAH. What time is your shoot at?

IAN. Is there someone else?

SARAH. Who do you think the someone might be?

IAN. Whoever you are meeting now? Whoever just called?

Whoever you are wearing this sexy stuff for?

SARAH. Ian. I'm auditioning.

IAN. Let me hold you.

She lets him. He smells her hair. He grinds against her.

Can you feel that?

SARAH. Nought to sixty in five seconds. You should be on *Top Gear*.

IAN. Do you want to talk to me?

Do you want to tell me things?

I felt so lucky when I found you. Feel so –

SARAH. Ian.

IAN. Touch me. Fuck it. Touch me.

Please.

She does so.

SARAH. There can't be two of us not moving.

In any direction. We have to do something. Change something.

He pushes her hand away.

IAN. What kind of change are you after?

SARAH. I don't know. We should talk.

Silence.

She holds out her hand for his camera.

IAN. No way.

SARAH. Please. I just want one of you.

IAN. Why?

SARAH. It's the way you're looking at me.

IAN. It's on automatic. Just point and press.

SARAH. But will it be art?

IAN. Depends on the story behind it.

SARAH. Is that what it's all about?

IAN. Absofuckinlutely.

SARAH. Ian?

IAN. Yes?

SARAH. You didn't find me. I found you.

She takes a photograph.

Scene Three

Dublin Airport. Early morning.

A coffee kiosk. ALICE *is serving.*

NEIL. A coffee, please.

ALICE. What kind?

NEIL. Emm – (*His phone is ringing.*)

ALICE. We got Cappuccino, Frappuchino, Mochochino, Chocochino (though that's not technically coffee).

Latte, Espresso, Machiato, Americano / (not selling too well these days).

NEIL. Just a regular coffee. / Hello?

ALICE. Black – White – De-caf – Fairtrade?

NEIL. Jim – how are you? Black Fairtrade, please.

ALICE. If you get a Tall Fairtrade you get a free muffin of your choice.

NEIL. Tall but no muffin. / Yeah, yeah?

ALICE. Your loss.

NEIL. Jim – Sorry. What? I am not a fucking car crash.

Ah – OK. A UN convoy is a bit of an exaggeration. No, we didn't make it back to Nyala. We met the fucking Janjaweed. If Tanya said that, it's a crock of shit. We have enough testimony between us to do a piece on Internally Displaced Persons – if that's how you want to proceed – but Jim, Jim – reconsider my material. It's scorched earth practically fucking live. Come on. I know what interests you. If it's too graphic for the news there's definitely a special in it. Yeah? Will you call me back?

Talk to you then. (*He hangs up.*) Fuck.

ALICE. Have a serviette, you're sweating.

NEIL. Thanks. (*He wipes his face.*)

ALICE. Hope it's not some nasty disease?

NEIL. Don't worry.

ALICE. Where are you coming from?

NEIL. Africa.

ALICE. Alas poor continent. Nobody cares.

NEIL. You think so?

ALICE. My uncle went to Uganda to do some teaching work.

After a couple of weeks he was found dead in his room, his brains oozing out his ears. It could have been a bug or it could have been Kony.

We just got the body bag. (*Handing him his coffee.*)

He dials a number.

Two euro and eighty cents.

He hands her some coins.

NEIL. Hello hello, I'm back.

I've got to talk to you.

I can't stop thinking about you.

Do you think of me?

And change your voice message.

Say something nice on it.

Call me – call me.

ZOË *enters. He turns around.*

ZOË. Hey.

NEIL. What are you doing here?

ZOË. What do you think?

NEIL. Sorry sorry – was about to ring. / I have my phone in my hand.

ZOË. You've put me through hell.

The station rang. Said they'd lost contact with you.

NEIL. God, I'm sorry. I wasn't lost though.

ZOË. I had to ring Jim on Monday to find that out.

NEIL. Fuck. Sorry.

ZOË. You've been drinking.

NEIL. One or two.

ZOË. Smells like five or six.

You're sweating.

NEIL. My gut is in a knot.

ZOË. Hungover?

NEIL. Not at all.

ZOË. You walked right past me back there.

NEIL. I didn't know you'd be here. I had no idea.

ZOË *breathes out.*

ZOË. I'd like a coffee too.

NEIL. OK. I'll get you one.

NEIL *returns to* ALICE.

Could I have a coffee, please? Sorry. Black Fairtrade.

ALICE. We're closed.

NEIL. But you just served me.

ALICE. I'm cleaning the machine.

NEIL. It's the morning. You shouldn't be closing.

ALICE. Says who? Is this an authoritarian regime?

NEIL. Just give me the muffin that was supposed to come with my Fairtrade coffee.

ALICE (*handing him a muffin*). Don't you think you had better get on with it? (*She pulls down her shutter.*)

NEIL *returns to* ZOË.

NEIL. Only muffins I'm afraid.

ZOË. Double Chocolate – my favourite.

Silence. She unwraps the muffin.

I kept the papers for you.

A bus crash on Dame Street, another factory goes belly up, *Big Brother*, Sven G. E.

A big pile of tat in a box.

NEIL. Maggie? How is she?

ZOË. Sullen, happy, sullen, happy. She's making macaroni for dinner.

NEIL. Sweet.

ZOË (*picking at the muffin*). I had a dream last night – our road had to be bombed.

All that was left was rubble – and I couldn't find you.

One of those dreams that upset you for the whole day?

She takes a bite.

Probably because I hadn't heard from you.

NEIL. It's a dream, Zoë.

ZOË. It looks bad out there.

NEIL. The world dithers. Again.

Talk less, act more.

ZOË. Pity you can't do the same.

NEIL. Look, I am sorry. I didn't know the desk called.

ZOË. You get lost and don't call me. What's going on?

NEIL. I didn't get lost. I was chasing a story. I got it – they still haven't aired it. / Small-time fucking.

ZOË. You're trouble, Neil – trouble to me – to Jim – to that girl who's your producer.

NEIL. Tanya.

ZOË. To our daughter.

NEIL *finishes his coffee – he wipes the sweat off his face.*

NEIL. Right, let's go if we are going.

ZOË. I went through your correspondence.

NEIL. What?

ZOË. Your Visa statements list hotels.

The Conrad? The Shelbourne? Nights you were supposed to be away working. Cards from a Miriam and others. There have been whispers in my office even.

NEIL. You shouldn't have done that, Zoë.

ZOË. If you won't tell me about yourself, I have to resort to investigation.

NEIL. So this is a grilling?

ZOË. Who is Miriam?

NEIL. You've met her. Miriam the girl from the Red Cross.

ZOË. Yes, that RTE party – you were talking about swimming in Croatia. No mention of the bloody war. And she laughed. She laughed at everything you said. Swimming in Croatia.

Are you fucking her?

NEIL. A relationship forged in conflict can take on – let's say proportions – but it doesn't / have to mean fucking.

ZOË. Neil there is a 'she', I know there is. I wake up each morning and feel like I've caught a freight train in my chest.

Is it Miriam? Because God help me I have her number – it was on the card – and I will ring and ask her myself.

NEIL. It is not Miriam.

ZOË (*takes out her phone and she presses a button*). Ringing.

NEIL. Hang up – It's not Miriam.

ZOË. Hi, is that Miriam?

NEIL (*grabs the phone out of her hand*). Miriam? Hi, Neil Devlin here. How are you – sorry, didn't realise it was four in the morning. No news. OK. You too. (*He hangs up.*)

What are you doing? She's in Washington.

ZOË. Something to hide?

NEIL. With her girlfriend.

ZOË. Right. So start telling the fucking truth for a change.

You make a living out of it – or do I have to ring every number in your address book?

Pause.

NEIL. There is someone. Yes.

ZOË. I have to corral you at the airport to hear it?

NEIL. I was going to tell you.

ZOË. When?

NEIL. I don't know.

Pause.

ZOË. Is it serious? I could possibly forgive less than serious.

NEIL. It has become serious.

ZOË. You love her?

NEIL *nods.*

Pause.

Jesus Christ. Jesus.

Pause.

ZOË *looks like she is going to be sick.*

Announcements bellow flight information. NEIL *moves to comfort her.*

Please don't touch me.

NEIL. I've been hurting you.

ZOË. You hurt everyone. You're a mess, Neil.

NEIL. We haven't been good for ages.

Why can't you face that?

We have no joy together.

ZOË. *You* haven't been trying – not 'we'. You talk about joy? I could kill you.

(*She stops – overwhelmed.*) I want to strike you. Please move away.

NEIL *takes a step back.*

Pause.

NEIL. What do you want me to do?

ZOË. You want to make your life with this person? What?

NEIL. I haven't thought it through.

ZOË. You had better start.

Silence.

We've been in limbo for about a year. Is that right?

(*She softens.*) Come on. It's fine. Just tell me.

NEIL. It's been about a year. Yes.

ZOË. You coward.

NEIL. Zoë.

ZOË. What have you been doing? Test-driving the new model?

You disgust me.

NEIL. I didn't have a plan, Zoë. It just happened.

I'll leave home.

ZOË. Yes, you will.

You don't have to. (*She controls herself.*)

No, you do. You have to get out. Go. I'm sick of it.

NEIL. OK.

Announcement for Arrivals interrupt.

Give me a couple of weeks. I will talk to Maggie this evening.

ZOË. Sixteen years dissolve at the airport. Life goes on.

If I hadn't said anything? What then, hmm?

Pause.

NEIL. I'll drive back if you like. Where is the car?

ZOË. Fuck off. Just fuck off.

ZOË *exits.*

NEIL *doesn't move.* ALICE *reappears and calls to* NEIL.

ALICE. So you've got another honey pot?

NEIL. What? (*He takes out his phone and dials.*)

ALICE. Another ladylove.

Another furry fun place.

Feel good about it? Doing the right thing?

NEIL. I'm fine. It will all be fine. (*He listens to the message service*: '*You have reached the voicemail of . . .* ')

Where are you?

He hangs up.

ALICE. OK. Whatever gets you through, Mr.

Scene Four

Audition.

SARAH *peers into bright lights.*

She steps forward a little.

DIRECTOR. If you could just stay on the blue mark, please.

SARAH. Oh yes. Sorry. (*She takes a step back.*)

DIRECTOR. Name, age, agent.

SARAH. Sarah Rafter. Thirty-four. The Actors Agency.

DIRECTOR. Never heard of it.

SARAH. It's a co-operative.

DIRECTOR. I see.

Profiles.

SARAH *turns slowly from right to left.*

Hurry it up a bit.

SARAH. Right. Sorry.

DIRECTOR. Smile.

SARAH. Sorry. I always find it difficult to smile if I've been told to.

Could you say something funny?

DIRECTOR. Just smile.

SARAH (*she smiles*). That does it for me every time.

DIRECTOR. Have you done any ads recently?

SARAH. I've made quite a few but not for a while.

DIRECTOR. I see. Any cereal commercials?

SARAH. I did turn down an ad for Nestlé once.

I'm not sure I'd do that now.

DIRECTOR. Principles need finance.

SARAH. Yes.

DIRECTOR. Talk to me a bit about a pash. A hobby or something you are passionate about. You have thirty seconds. Go.

SARAH. Emm . . . Ah ah – a pash? I . . . I'm passionate about acting.

I can say that, can't I?

DIRECTOR (*wearily*). Twenty-five seconds.

SARAH (*speed-talks*). I mean – acting is a vocation – that's not a cliché. It has to be.

Why would you choose such a life? I did burn. I still burn but I don't know how much longer without blowing out – you know?

It's like having an affair – you wait for the phone to ring –

SARAH*'s mobile rings.*

Bugger. Thought I'd turned it off.

DIRECTOR. You wait for the phone to ring – seven seconds –

SARAH *tries to ignore the ringing.*

SARAH (*talks even faster*). Yes. Frustration, bliss, pain, a kaleidoscope of possibility.

But is this an important job? If you consider the global nightmare that is elsewhere, I ask myself this question – does it matter? Do I?

DIRECTOR. Stop. OK. Do you have the sheet with the lines, yes?

SARAH. I know them.

Her phone bleeps loudly.

Sorry.

DIRECTOR. Well – I want you to deliver the monologue with that exact sense of discovery and passion.

SARAH. Ermm . . . right.

Right. Will I do it to you or to camera?

DIRECTOR. To me.

SARAH (*launches into the piece*). 'I work . . .

DIRECTOR. Don't forget you are walking the dog and the children are running ahead.

SARAH. You mean act it out?

DIRECTOR. Exactly.

SARAH. I'm not sure I'd be reaching for the milk while walking the dog.

DIRECTOR (*sighs*). You have a better idea no doubt?

SARAH. I could be playing with them – in the house, I mean . . .

DIRECTOR. So play.

SARAH. 'I work hard.

I play hard.

Sometimes I just need a 'Regular' day.

That's when I reach for the 'All-Brown'.

And some ice-cold milk –

Then I'm ready for anything life throws up.'

DIRECTOR. On the 'anything', the dog is pulling you.

I need to hear that.

Just go from 'I reach for . . . '

SARAH. OK. 'I reach for the 'All-Brown' and some ice-cold milk –

And I'm ready for aaaaaannnnnyyyything the dog throws up.'

DIRECTOR. Thank you.

SARAH. Sorry. Life throws up.

DIRECTOR. Thank you.

SARAH. Could I do that again?

DIRECTOR. Once was more than enough, goodbye.

The DIRECTOR *looks at his notes. He writes something. He looks up.*

SARAH. I made an awful mess of that.

I would really like to have another go.

DIRECTOR. Oh go on, just get out.

SARAH. Are you talking to me?

DIRECTOR. Yes. You. Has-been. Never has been.

Call yourself an actress? Out.

SARAH. What?

DIRECTOR. That was a terrible audition. Telephone ringing?
You fluffed it by talking shit. Acting is like having an affair?
Global nightmare? I've never heard such bollocks. Phuh.
Now go on, fuck off. Get a job in Tesco's.

SARAH. Look, you ass wipe. I've had a number of four-star
reviews in my time. I have come this close to being in a
film with Kevin Spacey. I'm trying to give these shitting
lines some dignity here.

If you don't like what I'm doing, blow it out your stinking –

DIRECTOR. Why you? You'll never work in this town again.

SARAH. Oh yeah? We'll see about that.

SARAH *takes out her finger as if it's a gun and shoots the*
DIRECTOR.

I am not an idiot. I just want to work.

I am not an idiot.

The DIRECTOR *dies horribly. The bullets making him
convulse as they hit.*

I am not an idiot.

Scene Five

A photographic studio.

IAN *is rolling up a lead while talking on his mobile. The place
is littered with paper cups and clothes bags.* ELSA *enters, also
talking on a mobile phone.*

ELSA (*laughs*). Yes.

IAN. Number Eight.

ELSA (*laughs*). Yes.

IAN. It's off –

ELSA (*laughs*). Yes.

IAN. No. No. The second right.

ELSA. I'll be there.

IAN. Right.

ELSA. How long?

IAN. How long?

> ELSA *stops laughing.* IAN *looks at her.*

ELSA. I'll think about it.

IAN. Bye.

ELSA. Bye.

> *They look at one another.*

> ELSA *smiles.*

IAN. Your taxi went missing in action.

> *Pause.*

ELSA. I'm not in a rush.

IAN. The wrong address and now . . .

ELSA. I get a chance to talk to you.

IAN. Oh. Oh right.

ELSA. That was Michael.

He recommends a champagne lunch after charity.

You up for it?

IAN. I've got to pack up here.

> ELSA *brings over some drinks. She looks around. The place is in bits.*

ELSA. We've left a massacre.

> *She starts to pick up the photo-shoot debris.*

> *She comes across some discarded Polaroids. She studies them.*

These are good. He can look bland in publicity shots.

What do Amnesty pay an hour?

IAN. Are you joking?

I get my expenses. You don't do this work for the fee.

ELSA. I'd like you to do some proper ones of Michael.

IAN. Right. Thank you . . . Sorry, I'm a little confused. Are
you Michael's assistant or . . . ?

ELSA. Elsa? Elsa. I'm the producer of *The MFCS*.

The Michael Farrell Cookery Show?

IAN. Make-up, wives, children, nannies, Amnesty.

I didn't know who was doing what.

ELSA. You assumed I was the dogsbody.

IAN. I'm just old and bitter.

ELSA. Saw that when the television cameras arrived.

IAN. The media confuses celebrities with politicians.

What does Michael Farrell know about human rights?

ELSA. Fuck all.

IAN. Exactly. It's just for the sake of a career.

ELSA. What part of 'Raising Awareness' offends?

IAN. You're what they call – The New Ireland.

ELSA. That's us. Apolitical and amoral. We believe in
Celebrity Chefs and Reality TV.

IAN. Reality TV makes me nauseous.

ELSA. Cultural stereotyping has the same effect on me. Can
I have these? (*Polaroids.*)

IAN. Yeah. Sure.

ELSA. So tell me about your social conscience?

IAN. What?

IAN *continues to pack up his equipment.*

ELSA. I saw your exhibition. The group one in The Gallery Of Photography.

IAN. You saw it? Oh right.

ELSA. It was hardcore. Spar Supermarkets – The Hidden Ireland.

The ethnic mix that serves the nation its milk and fags.

IAN. Well remembered.

ELSA. I bought the catalogue.

Some of the work – all you got was the narrative. Why no photograph?

IAN. The Africans didn't want to be photographed.

They get shit here even when they are legal.

But that's not really what it was about.

ELSA. So what was it about?

IAN. The changing face of the Emerald Isle.

ELSA. What's your next exhibition?

IAN. Look – my photography lies more in the pack-shot variety. Tins of peaches arranged in pyramids.

ELSA. That's crazy. Why?

IAN. I've got to pay the car tax.

ELSA. But you're talented.

IAN. That's very nice of you.

ELSA. I'm not trying to be nice. I could help you out of fringe territory.

IAN. I like fringe territory. I've been there quite a long time.

ELSA. It doesn't pay the bills, does it?

IAN. So who do you know?

ELSA. Me.

IAN *looks at her and laughs.*

IAN. You're funny.

ELSA. I'm bossy. My first school report said, 'Elsa is domineering the boys.'

IAN. Where did you get a name like Elsa?

ELSA. Are you chatting me up?

IAN. I'm curious.

ELSA. It's the same thing.

IAN. I am called Ian after my father.

He was called Ian after his father and so on. See. It's a story.

ELSA. That's how people fall in love.

IAN. How?

ELSA. Each other's stories.

I'm called Elsa – after the lion. The TV series *Born Free*?

IAN. I like it. I like that story.

ELSA. Tell me another story about you?

IAN. I am forty. I have an apartment in Ballsbridge and covet my neighbour's Aston Martin V8. I couldn't live without my Hasselblad.

I teach on occasion but my last lecture, 'Daguerreotype to Digital', sent my students into a coma. I'm not 'down' enough with the 'Yoof' apparently. Favourite item of clothing – a Fat Freddy T-shirt that my girlfriend likes to wear to bed.

ELSA. Girlfriend?

IAN. Yeah.

ELSA. What's her name?

IAN. Sarah.

She's an actress.

ELSA. Would I have seen her in anything?

IAN. Not yet.

ELSA. She needs a break too?

IAN. She was in a production of *A Doll's House* last year.

The toughest critic of them all said –

'Sarah Rafter is exquisite.'

ELSA. So why isn't she known?

IAN. It was in Limerick. Tell me your story.

ELSA. I'm twenty-five. Single. I have my own production company, documentaries about Italian chippers in Dublin etc., then *The Michael Farrell Cookery Show*. I discovered him in a restaurant in Kinsale, flambéing and regaling diners with charming tales of domesticity. I couldn't live without casual sex and my favourite item is a Sekonda watch given to me for my tenth birthday.

IAN. All on the one breath. I'm impressed.

ELSA. I'm very good – orally.

IAN (*chokes on his drink*). Pheeww.

ELSA *picks up her bag and pulls out a hanky.*

ELSA. You need a cloth or a tissue?

IAN. I seem to have made a mess of myself.

ELSA (*dabbing his mouth*). It's clean.

IAN. Are you chatting me up?

ELSA. Why don't you kiss me?

IAN. Too old for lunging.

ELSA. You've never been unfaithful?

IAN. I have but not to Sarah.

ELSA. How many years?

IAN. Ten.

ELSA. Wow.

Can't imagine a decade with someone. Snore.

IAN. Maybe you've never been in love before.

ELSA. 'In love' doesn't last.

IAN. You know this because?

ELSA. I have parents.

IAN. The alternatives to monogamy are depressing.

ELSA. Interesting similarity with – monotony.

IAN. How did we get started on this?

ELSA. 'O go my man.'

IAN. What?

ELSA. It's an anagram of 'Monogamy'.

IAN. Right.

ELSA. You need a change of scenery.

IAN. You're funny.

ELSA. If you are not coming to me – I am coming to you.

IAN *laughs.*

Scene Six

A hotel room. Clothes strewn – NEIL is hunched over a small coffee table, typing. He has a towel around his waist. He is talking on his mobile.

NEIL. Fair enough – If you are worried – we can go to the wide shot there –

It's the burnt corpse of a child – but you can't tell what it is in the wide. Well yes – if you freeze-frame but even then it looks like a black blob –

Nah Jim – it'll lose impact if we sanitise the thing completely. OK. I suggest we intercut the footage of the blood river (by the group of executed men and boys) with that of the Janjaweed arsing around. That's pretty chilling. Mmm? I'm not sure about the aid effort – do without, I say. Let's aim to provoke a strong response – yes, that's what I'm thinking, fucking bleak, yeah? Good.

Is Tanya back?

Did she get anyone to do the interviews?

Right.

Edit suite at three.

OK Jim.

He hangs up.

(*Shouts to off.*) Yesss. Hey – I'm back in business.

The special is going out on the nine o'clock.

SARAH *enters. She is wrapped in a large towel.*

SARAH. I thought it was too offensive for the nation's viewing?

NEIL. Shots of massacred children are unacceptable but a few judicious cuts – sorted. Access and exclusivity – no editor is going to turn their nose up at that. Tanya's refugee camps – it's good but everyone's got that. No one, not even the BBC has got stuff like I have.

SARAH (*moving towards bathroom*). No one has got stuff like I have.

She throws her towel at him as she disappears.

NEIL *follows but watches from without.*

NEIL. Oh man.

I love you. I love you. I love you.

Oh no. Don't put on the knicks. No.

Not the bra. Bye bye.

Agghh, I hate the tights.

Not the dress. Noooooooooooooo.

SARAH *re-enters, dressed.*

SARAH. My boots?

NEIL. Over there. Nearly broke my neck on them.

SARAH *kisses him and sits to put her boots on.*

NEIL *watches her slide her boots on.*

Don't move.

SARAH. Hmm?

She stops.

NEIL. That's the picture. I thought about this moment. Dreamt about it.

You'd be sitting there and I'd be safe.

We met the Janjaweed. Thirty scary fuckers on horseback. Laden with stuff. Cattle and goats in tow.

Me and Pete – out of the van – camera on the bonnet. Camera running. I proffer a bottle of water. The leader gets off his horse and approaches like I am Ursula Andress in *She*. He takes the water – knocks it back – it rolls down his neck – the rest of his mates get off their horses – posture and smile for the camera – Janjaweed equivalent of mooning. They ask for nothing – they let us go. We drive. Pete says 'Oh fuck.' A settlement in the distance. Smoke. We get closer – unmistakable stench – the buzz of flies like high-voltage power lines. We step into an unspeakable scene of savagery. The Janjaweed – they have no feelings. Blood, limbs, fire, kiddies with their skulls crushed. We have followed in their wake.

It's the money shot and I can't believe my luck.

SARAH. Luck?

NEIL. We're trying not to gag – this dour Welsh cameraman – tears running as he looks through the eyepiece – we hear the sound of aircraft – shit ourselves – there is nowhere to hide.

We get in the van and drive like the clappers – but my first thought was of you – I had to get back for you – that was very clear. This shocked me – more than the threat of the gunships – more than the corpses piled high. Men, women, children already rotting in the sun.

He buries his head in her.

I need you.

SARAH. God.

NEIL. Run away with me.

SARAH. Neil . . .

NEIL. If you won't – I'll become an alcoholic.

SARAH. You are one.

NEIL. I won't work, I won't wash, I'll have itchy pants.

SARAH. Be serious.

NEIL. I've left Zoë.

SARAH. What?

NEIL. I told her everything.

SARAH. You did?

NEIL. I told her I was in love. I had to leave.

SARAH. You said my name? She knows Ian for God's sake.

NEIL. Course I didn't. She has her own ideas though.

It's over. It's done. At the airport.

SARAH. That was cruel.

NEIL. Will we talk about cruelty? Fucking me in your bed?

Washing the come off your sheets? / Phone calls? Hotels?

SARAH. OK OK, enough.

NEIL. I love you. You love me.

SARAH *moves away.*

SARAH. But why now?

NEIL. You're a great fuck.

SARAH. You're taking a hammer to your life for a decent blow-job?

NEIL. Christing Jesus – haven't you been listening to me?

I love you.

SARAH. You've been in a bad place – you just want out.

I don't want to be your fire escape.

NEIL. You're not my fire escape. You're my future.

I love you. Hear me.

SARAH. And I love you.

But we don't really know each other. We don't know one another's toilet habits –

You wouldn't love me if you knew me.

NEIL. Ah for fuck's sake . . .

SARAH. It's important.

NEIL. OK. Tell me the worst.

SARAH. I'm out of work, which makes me miserable, vaguely desperate, and sometimes a little paranoid.

NEIL. It's the same for a foreign correspondent.

What else?

SARAH. I have a tendency towards pettiness.

NEIL. How bad can it be?

SARAH. The kitchen – Ian insists on using separate knives for everything. He is incredibly particular about it. We must use the bread knife for the bread, onion knife for the onions, cheese knife for the cheese, etc. So when he goes out, it gives me tremendous pleasure to cut carrots with the bread knife. Do you understand? Incompatibility reveals itself through co-habitation.

NEIL. I have no interest in the kitchen. Hit me again.

SARAH. OK, what about my driving? How do you rate it?

NEIL. Good. Sometimes you are overly cautious but . . .

SARAH. You see, that's what I mean. In a year's time you will be screaming at me to enter a roundabout.

I couldn't bear that to happen to us. I'm scared we will lose what we have. It's my only joy.

NEIL. It will be different. I'm determined to do it right this time.

Now listen to me. I can't do anything without you any more. I want to know you're in my life.

There is a knock at the door.

ALICE. Room service?

NEIL (*shouting*). Not now, thank you.

> ALICE *lets herself in. She has a bundle of towels and toilet rolls in her arms and a lollipop in her mouth.*

ALICE. Room service.

NEIL. I said not now.

ALICE. Sorry, I didn't hear you. Carry on, carry on.

> Towels and toilet roll. I won't be a minute.

> *She's gone.*

SARAH. But say if it hurts?

NEIL. Of course it will hurt. Get ready for devastation.

SARAH. I'm afraid of pain.

> I've spent a lifetime dodging it. I don't even like playing characters that suffer. 'All-Brown' is as much as I can cope with.

NEIL. Sarah – it will be more painful if you look back and you didn't jump.

SARAH. I've been living a lie for so long I don't know how to do truth.

> And goodbye seems rather abrupt.

NEIL. Put it in a letter. Write it down. It helps.

> If you don't give me an answer in one minute I am going to throw myself out this window. OK?

> *He moves toward the window.*

> ALICE *re-enters.*

SARAH. Wait – If I leave Ian? Happy? Will I make you happy?

ALICE. Happy?

> Phhhhhh.

> You think it will be any different with him?

> But someday you'll find a nice little hatred growing – no – he will hate you more because he loves you more and by

that time you'll have a little house together and a little car and maybe a – (*She cradles an imaginary baby.*) or maybe a dog.

And then she'll catch you fucking the au pair and, boy, is she gonna screw your ass – take you for every dog hair you got.

What are you looking at? (*She threatens* SARAH *with the lolly.*)

You think it's OK to just look?

SARAH. You're talking to me. You just were talking.

ALICE. I'm talking to him, Pokémon.

NEIL. Could you just leave, please?

ALICE. Good luck in Happy Town, you pack of shits.

She exits. They look at one another.

NEIL. Fifty-seven seconds, fifty-eight, fifty-nine.

SARAH. Promise me it will be different with you.

Scene Seven

Studio. ELSA *and* IAN *are making love. It is not pretty.*

ELSA. Yes, yes, come on, that's good, yeah.

IAN. Wait . . . wait . . . don't move.

ELSA. You're not gonna.

IAN. Be still.

ELSA. I'm still.

IAN. You're amazing – you know that.

ELSA *moves again.*

ELSA. Yep.

IAN. Whoah whoo oh.

The doorbell rings.

ELSA. That's the taxi.

IAN. Fuck – rugby tackle, income tax, church, yes, no, fax, photocopy, paper, jam, Tesco's, hailstones, shit, shit.

Sorry. God, sorry. Caught it.

IAN *stands there awkwardly as* ELSA *straightens her clothes.*

ELSA. Don't worry about it.

IAN. Hmm? Yes . . . listen, sorry. I can eh do something for you if –

Just give me five minutes, yeah? Maybe ten –

ELSA. It's cool. Really. (*She pulls on her undies.*)

The bell rings again.

IAN. Right.

ELSA. One of us should get the door?

IAN. Yes. I will. (*Pulling up his trousers.*)

IAN *hobbles to the door.*

Shit. Ehh OK.

He scours about wildly for a rag or something.

ELSA. It's fine. I'll do it. (*She exits to the driver.*)

IAN. Right.

He looks around then opts to wipe his hands on his trousers.

ELSA *re-enters.*

ELSA. He will wait a few minutes. No panic.

ELSA *deftly organises herself. She sprays some perfume.*

Hands him a tissue.

IAN *hovers awkwardly.*

The actress should be giving you loads. I think you're hot.

IAN. Hot. Right eh – sorry about – it's been a while.

ELSA. Difficulties with the actress?

IAN. After ten years it's not called 'difficulties', it's called everyday.

ELSA. Oh dear.

IAN *struggles to contain the urge to run.*

It's OK, you know – really it is.

IAN. Yeah, sure. Everything is grand.

ELSA. I'm having difficulties with my boy too.

I love knowing I've punished him and he never has to know. Don't let it get you down.

Pause. ELSA *smiles. She walks towards the door.*

Sorry, I have to run like this – Michael will be wondering where I am.

IAN. Champagne after charity. That's right. (*He laughs.*) That's a good one. (*His laugh trails off.*)

ELSA. Will you email me the contact sheets tonight?

IAN. Of course.

ELSA. Goodbye then. (*She kisses him briefly on the lips.*)

You're sweet. You really are.

IAN. Yeah. Sweet. Cool. Cool.

She exits.

Cool? Shit, shit, shit.

Scene Eight

NEIL *and* ZOË*'s living room.*

MAGGIE (*fifteen*) *is in her pyjamas. She is sitting in front of the TV, eating dry cereal out of the box* (*Sugar Puffs*)*. She picks at a guitar.*

MTV rages. Magazines are at her feet and evidence of a recent pedicure. NEIL *enters.*

NEIL. Hello.

She doesn't answer.

Hello?

MAGGIE. Yeah. Heard you the first time. Hello.

NEIL. Sorry, sweetheart, I got delayed.

The place looks different. Did Mummy move things?

MAGGIE. Yes, Dad. Last year. We moved the TV.

NEIL. Did we?

Turn it down, Maggie.

MAGGIE. You can't come back after two weeks and tell me what to do.

NEIL. I can. Please.

She turns the TV down.

MAGGIE. The macaroni has turned to cement.

NEIL. We'll get a takeaway.

MAGGIE. I'm sorted. (*She shakes the cereal box at him.*)

How was Africa?

NEIL. Do you really want to know?

MAGGIE. Your report has just aired.

NEIL. What did you think?

MAGGIE. It was sick. Are you trying to give us all nightmares?

NEIL. Just trying to break through the atrocity fatigue, darling.

MAGGIE. Yeah well, bet half the country reached for their remote control.

Re-runs of *Friends* is on Network Two.

NEIL. Where's Mummy?

MAGGIE. Went to bed with a headache. She's been waiting too.

NEIL. I've been in the studio, darling. I was working the piece till the last minute.

Do I get a kiss?

MAGGIE. No.

NEIL tries to put his arms around her.

Get off me or I'll call ChildLine.

NEIL. That isn't funny.

MAGGIE. Neither is burnt macaroni.

NEIL. I'll make it up to you.

MAGGIE. Whatever. Like you're around.

ZOË enters. She is carrying a handful of files and books.

ZOË. I heard you come in.

NEIL. Feeling better?

ZOË. Are you?

He nods.

I'm going to try and get some work done.

Do you want some food?

NEIL. No thanks.

ZOË. You've eaten?

She dumps her work materials down and moves toward the kitchen.

NEIL. Not hungry.

ZOË. OK. So where's this Macaroni Cheese?

MAGGIE. Bin.

ZOË. I was looking forward to that.

MAGGIE. Weren't we all? (*She picks at a chord.*)

ZOË. Maggie.

MAGGIE. What?

ZOË. I don't want to be looking at this mess in the morning.

MAGGIE. You won't be.

NEIL. What's all this?

MAGGIE. It's beauty stuff.

ZOË. Maggie has decided she needs to change her image.

NEIL. Why?

MAGGIE. You've got to sex up to make it in the music business.

NEIL. Says who?

MAGGIE. Nobody says. I know.

ZOË. Welcome to my world.

NEIL. Don't you have to get a gig first? To make it in the music business . . .

MAGGIE. What would you know?

I've played gigs at school. You never get to them.

NEIL. I have to work, Maggie. It's not my fault.

Who do you think paid for that guitar? Your computer? Your iPod?

MAGGIE. So it's all about money?

NEIL. No but my work is a fact of life.

ZOË. I work too.

MAGGIE. Mum never misses anything I do.

NEIL. At least you have one of us. My parents never came to anything of mine.

MAGGIE. Dad – I don't want to hear about the Hovis days. Like – yawn.

NEIL. Right. Sorry. Nothing. I know nothing.

MAGGIE. Thank you.

NEIL. How's the work, Zoë?

ZOË. I've reading to do. But it's mainly artwork / to look at.

I'm a bit behind.

MAGGIE. Why didn't you call us? When you were away?

NEIL. I didn't get a chance, Maggie.

MAGGIE. You get a chance to talk to your work – but not us?

That's pretty weird.

NEIL. I'll phone every day the next time.

MAGGIE. It's just so hard to get your attention, Dad.

Maybe if someone macheted us.

Or dropped a bomb on us.

She mimes a noose around her throat and pulls it.

She puts on a cartoon voice.

I'm dying, Daddy.

She deepens her voice as NEIL.

Just wait till I get my microphone.

NEIL. You're very important to me.

MAGGIE. Dad. You have no feelings.

NEIL. What? What / are you saying?

MAGGIE. You don't even love us any more.

NEIL. Of course I love you. I love you and Mummy / very much.

ZOË. Leave me out of it.

MAGGIE. That's not true. You haven't called in two weeks. Mum is back on Prozac / and you haven't taken your jacket off yet.

ZOË. Maggie – They are vitamins.

Have you been / going through my things?

NEIL *takes his jacket off.*

MAGGIE. What will happen to us?

We will still be here. We always have been. Waiting.

NEIL. Don't panic. Everything will be OK.

ZOË. Darling. Your father and I have decided that it's best if . . .

Pause.

Your father has decided that it's best if he lives somewhere else.

MAGGIE. No way.

Silence.

Is it true?

NEIL. It might be better for everyone.

MAGGIE. Who is it better for?

NEIL. I'm not going anywhere tonight.

ZOË. Tell her why you're leaving us?

NEIL. You're upsetting Maggie.

ZOË. I'm upsetting Maggie? You're upsetting us all.

NEIL. You're pushing this, Zoë. Just back off.

ZOË. Back off? You're / telling me to back –

MAGGIE. Shut up shut up shut up.

She stands up.

Isn't anybody going to fight for one another?

ZOË. He doesn't want that.

MAGGIE. I've done everything to keep this / family together.

NEIL. Darling. It's not about fighting for anyone. It's more complicated than that.

I've met someone. / And though I love you and Mummy.

MAGGIE. What?

NEIL. It's different.

MAGGIE. I feel sick.

ZOË. Daddy has been seeing this person.

MAGGIE. Are you sleeping with her?

NEIL *hesitates.*

Well?

NEIL. Yes.

MAGGIE. I hate you. / You pervert.

NEIL. I'll always be your daddy.

MAGGIE. Fuck off. You're insane.

MAGGIE *runs off.*

ZOË. You were supposed to love me.

You said it in front of sixty of our friends and family –

Something along the lines of . . . My life will be a better one bonded to yours. Even my father cried.

I worried about you every night you were away.

Northern Ireland. The Lebanon. Bosnia. Kosovo. Mogadishu.

Does it mean nothing?

What did I do wrong?

I could write the book by now.

Chapter One – don't panic, he may remember he loves you.

Chapter Two – lose twenty pounds and promise to swallow from now on.

Or Chapter Three – try not to fucking die.

NEIL. I'm so sorry.

NEIL *puts his arms around* ZOË.

ZOË. I've put my whole life into you. Keeping you vertical at the best of times. What have you ever done for me?

NEIL. I never asked you to martyr yourself.

ZOË. You needed me.

NEIL. Things have changed.

ZOË. That's how you sum up the last sixteen years?

We have Maggie. That hasn't changed.

NEIL. I'll do what you want me to do.

Pause.

This could be a new beginning for both of us.

ZOË. God – you talk bollocks. I'm the only one who sees that.

At least I don't have to worry you're going to make this 'new' one happy.

You make life shit for everyone.

NEIL (*explodes*). Why don't you shut up to fuck?

Shut fucking up. Fuck up.

She exits. MAGGIE*'s music blasts from overhead.*

Scene Nine

Four a.m.

IAN *is looking at contact sheets.*

SARAH *enters with a letter in her hand. She is wearing PJ bottoms and an ancient Fat Freddy T-shirt.*

SARAH. It's four o'clock.

IAN. I've been working. Don't feel like going to bed.

SARAH. That's a lot of hours for very little return.

IAN. Story of my life. What's up with you?

SARAH. Can't sleep.

Is that Michael Farrell?

IAN (*handing her the contact sheets*). Yeah. Mr Perfect.

SARAH. His wife and children too?

IAN. Yep. This man knows about photo opportunities.

SARAH. They look so wholesome.

Roses around the door and the smell of baking.

He'll probably turn out to be a wife beater.

IAN. Don't be ridiculous.

SARAH. Well, he's twenty-eight and has four kids. There's something of the feral about him.

IAN. Did you have bread last night when you came in?

SARAH. Hmm? I might have done.

What's the problem?

IAN. You undercut the bread and then you used the bread knife for the butter – I have asked you.

SARAH. File it under war crimes against Ian Fenton.

IAN. Don't use it as a way to start an argument.

SARAH. You started it.

IAN. What I mean is – when things happen – we should say them to one another. Transparency. You know?

SARAH. Transparency over bread – OK.

She hands him back the contact sheets.

IAN *looks at the letter in* SARAH's *hand. He looks at her. He decides to say nothing. He looks back at the contact sheets. He writes some numbers in a notebook. After a moment:*

The *Alice* job – I'm going to take it.

IAN *listens to something.*

What?

IAN. The sound of your 'Horse called Dignity' bolting.

SARAH. Ian. I've said it before. You are not the funniest man I have ever met.

I didn't get the ad, I have nothing work-wise on the table, my bank manager thinks it's a good idea.

Besides it will give us . . .

IAN. What?

SARAH. Space.

IAN. Our problem isn't space, Sarah.

There's tumbleweed between us. (*Pause.*)

I tried to talk to you yesterday.

SARAH. It's not about apportioning blame.

IAN. Of course it is.

Pause.

I need to be honest with you.

SARAH. I haven't been as transparent as I should.

IAN. Let me say something first.

SARAH. This is important.

IAN. Before / you say –

SARAH. Our relationship is a corpse.

It's rotting, it stinks.

No amount of trying / will resuscitate it.

IAN. I was with someone last night.

SARAH. What did / you say?

IAN. Did you rehearse that speech?

SARAH. Yes. I did. What did you say? You were with someone?

IAN. Yes.

A one-night stand.

SARAH. Oh. / Oh . . . well . . . I . . .

IAN. Sarah. Sarah.

In my defence – I was trying to reach out to you.

My confidence is shot to shit.

Yes, things are not good. Bad. They are bad.

But maybe somehow we could find a way?

SARAH. Are you serious?

IAN. I thought I could shake things up. Do something like you said.

SARAH. Fucking someone wasn't what I had in mind.

IAN. It meant nothing. I was thinking of you.

SARAH. You were thinking of me while you were fucking someone else?

IAN. Stranger things.

Aren't you going to say anything? Abuse me?

SARAH. Why?

IAN. I'd feel better.

SARAH. OK. I'm punished.

IAN. Why aren't you upset?

I fucked someone. I sucked someone's tits. I came like a train.

You hurting yet?

Silence.

Come on. I've told you mine – so you tell me yours.

SARAH. This is hard.

IAN. I've made it easy.

He sees the letter.

Is that for me?

SARAH. It doesn't matter now. It's stupid.

IAN. What could you possibly say in a letter that you couldn't say to my face?

SARAH. Just forget it.

He grabs the letter.

Give it back.

IAN. I'm reading it.

SARAH. I forbid you to.

IAN. You forbid me to?

I'm opening it.

SARAH. No you're not.

IAN. Yes I am.

SARAH. No.

IAN. Yes.

He opens the letter.

She snatches it and tears it up.

He tries to pick up the letter but she kicks the pieces out of his way.

Fucking stop with it, Sarah.

He grabs her and grapples her to the ground.

SARAH. Get off me.

IAN. Don't bite. Aggghhhh.

SARAH. I'm having an affair.

IAN. I fucking know you are.

You were going to tell me in a letter, like I'm . . . I'm some kind of overdue library book?

SARAH. I feel stupid.

IAN. I sing like a canary and you write a letter.

Why don't I just piece these together and help you out here.

He picks up a piece of the letter. Reads.

'Support your . . . and creative needs . . . ' What's that word?

SARAH. Stop.

IAN. How long has it been going on?

Three months.

SARAH *nods.*

Six months?

She nods.

A year?

SARAH. Yes.

IAN (*throwing the letter at her*). Who are you?

SARAH. I ask myself that question.

IAN. You said you loved me yesterday?

SARAH. I know.

IAN. Was it a lie?

SARAH *picks up bits of the letter.*

Stop.

SARAH. Ask me.

IAN. Do I know him?

SARAH. His name is Neil Devlin.

IAN. Wait – his wife? Zoë. She published the / catalogue for Spar. The Hidden Ireland.

SARAH. Yeah. Yes.

IAN. That atrocity tourist?

You're fucking him?

SARAH. It's more than fucking. Don't be reductive.

IAN. Me? Reductive? You've been diminishing me for months.

My spiritual height is all of two foot.

SARAH. Blame me if it makes you feel better.

But it's no good between / us any more.

IAN. Oh man. Did you cop off with him at my exhibition?

SARAH. I met him that night, yes.

IAN. So . . . what? You swapped phone numbers / under our noses?

SARAH. I didn't want to hurt you. It's why it's taken me so long . . .

IAN. Does this mean you are leaving?

Are you leaving me?

SARAH. Why would you want me?

IAN. Because I love you, you silly fucking bitch.

SARAH. It's too late.

IAN. Don't say that. It's not too late.

If I forgave you? You forgave me? Do you think? It could be exciting. We could talk to a counsellor. Maybe we should have a baby.

SARAH. It's gone, Ian.

IAN. I won't let you go.

SARAH. You don't have a choice.

IAN. I've been your life. You 'found' me. Finder's keepers.

SARAH. I told you it's gone.

IAN. You can't tell me it's gone without giving me a chance.

SARAH. Actually I can.

IAN. Jesus. Do you hate me? Have we / become such strangers?

SARAH. Of course I don't hate you.

IAN. Is it because he's famous? Are you a star fucker?

SARAH. Ian – that's just crass.

IAN. So why? Why is it gone? It's love you're talking about? Yes?

SARAH. I could say things that would be hurtful. What is the point in that?

IAN. Say them. Say the most hurtful things. Say them.

Come on. COME ON. Why?

Why? Why? Why? Why?

WHY? / WHY? WHY?

SARAH. I don't like the way you talk – I'm not interested in what you have to say – I don't like your smell – You bore me – you annoy me – I don't like your jokes – I don't like that you never pay the bills on time – I don't like that you think the bathroom is self-cleaning – I don't like your past – I don't want your future – I don't like you touching me – I hate your obsession with the right cutlery – I hate your critiques on my driving – If I'm going to struggle all my life I don't want it to be with you.

Living with you is torture because I just don't love you.

Pause.

IAN. So. You don't hate me. Thank you.

Scene Ten

Darkness. We can just about see NEIL. *He is awake – shaking.*
There is half a bottle of whiskey by his feet.

MAGGIE *enters.*

MAGGIE. Dad?

Pause.

NEIL. Hello darling.

Pause.

Turn on the little lamp.

She does so.

MAGGIE. I heard you shouting.

NEIL. Sorry. Nightmare. (*He drinks.*)

MAGGIE. Is this your new bed? (*Referring to the couch.*)

NEIL. Yeah.

MAGGIE. Comfortable?

NEIL. Not.

Pause.

MAGGIE. What does 'Kewa roota' mean?

Pause.

NEIL. Why?

MAGGIE. You were shouting it.

Pause.

NEIL. My fixer kept saying it. It means 'blood rivers'.

Pause.

MAGGIE. Right.

Pause.

Smells like a brewery in here.

NEIL. Open a window.

MAGGIE *moves toward the window. She looks out.*

MAGGIE. It's still dark.

NEIL. Not for much longer.

Pause.

MAGGIE. If I go to bed – will you be here – in the morning?

NEIL. Yes. I will. I'll make my famous pancakes if you like.

MAGGIE. I like.

MAGGIE *picks up her guitar. Looks at it. Look at him.*

Play something, Daddy.

She hands him the guitar and she curls up beside him sucking her thumb.

NEIL *strums very softly and sings a verse of 'Ain't No Cure For Love' (Leonard Cohen).*

Interval.

Scene Eleven

ZOË *is making a video of herself for internet dating.*

ZOË. Hi. I'm Zoë. I'm a thirty-five-year-old mother of one.

I like cooking, gardening and current affairs. In that order.

I work for a publishing company.

Pause.

That doesn't sound very interesting. (*Sighs.*)

But it is . . .

Pause.

We were told to tell an amusing story about ourselves . . . well . . .

Well, I won the title of Little Miss Dumdreg in 1981.

It's hardly what you call winning a beauty contest.

You were judged on personality and skills.

I know, revolutionary thinking in a one-horse town.

One girl did card tricks, another clicked out the National Anthem on dessert spoons. I played 'You Fill Up My Senses' on the tin whistle.

(*She holds up a battered tin whistle.*) This is the tin whistle.

She plays a couple of bars falteringly.

But my mother – God. My hair.

She insisted I get it cut before the competition.

She said I had to because I looked like King Herod.

So I was shorn. People called me sonny then.

I mean, what do you think that does to a kid?

Anyway, I won.

Look – I'm looking for love and commitment.

Time wasters need not apply.

Scene Twelve

Morning. A bare room.

Boxes and black plastic bags.

NEIL *is typing on his laptop. He is in his boxer shorts.*

We hear SARAH *laughing from off.* NEIL *looks up.*

NEIL. Sarah?

She stops laughing. She shouts from off.

SARAH. Are the bags of clothes downstairs?

NEIL. There are black plastic bags. What's in them I don't know.

SARAH *enters. She is half-dressed. She watches* NEIL *for some moments.*

She has a CD case in her hand.

Were you on the phone?

SARAH. No. I was – (*She stops. Laughs.*)

I was unpacking and . . . and . . .

NEIL. Yes?

SARAH. I – found – Ian's – Pink – Floyd – CD.

She laughs again.

NEIL. Sarah – I can't understand you.

She calms herself.

SARAH. I found Ian's Pink Floyd CD in my *Greatest Hits of Burt Bacharach.*

I've been thinking about his face.

She laughs and becomes incoherent.

He's so particular about things in their right place.

NEIL. Right?

SARAH. That's all.

She looks around the room. She breathes out.

It will be fine.

Once we get a couch.

NEIL. Maybe some pictures?

SARAH. Do you have any?

NEIL. They were all Zoë's. You?

SARAH. A framed photograph of me at Sarah Bernhardt's grave.

Pause.

NEIL. Great.

SARAH (*peering into bags*). Cushions add colour.

When we get the couch.

NEIL. I hate cushions.

SARAH. OK. Let's not have what we hate.

She goes to another black bag.

The fan in the bathroom doesn't work.

And we'll need a washing machine.

NEIL. Ah no. We'll be fine.

SARAH. Neil. We have to have a washing machine.

NEIL. OK. Then we do.

SARAH (*looking through the bags*). I can't find anything.

The sound of drum practice.

Shit. The kid next door.

SARAH *moves to the window. They look at one another.*

He continues to work. SARAH *continues to look out.*

At least there's a nice view.

NEIL. The television mast or the motorway?

SARAH. No. Out here.

NEIL. If you like looking at other people's washing.

SARAH *turns away.*

Sarah?

SARAH. Mmm hmm?

She moves back to a bag.

She roots through the clothes.

NEIL. What?

SARAH. I don't know. Nothing.

NEIL. Come here.

SARAH. In a minute.

The drumbeat gets a little louder.

SARAH *finds a pair of jeans.*

NEIL *stops working.*

If I scream 'Shut it' out the window, he might get the message.

NEIL. You'll frighten the pigeons.

The drumbeat breaks through.

Saturday fucking morning. The kid is a genius.

SARAH. Oh God.

They look at one another and burst out laughing.

NEIL. Please come here.

I love you.

SARAH (*moving to him*). Are you sure you don't miss . . .

NEIL. My own study, bathroom as big as this flat, patio garden?

Course not.

Fuck. Poor Zoë. I hope she meets someone.

SARAH. Isn't it funny how terrifying it is to leave?

NEIL. I wish it was funny.

SARAH (*looks at the boxes by his feet*). You could unpack some of your stuff maybe?

NEIL. I will.

SARAH. It's an emotional see-saw. The things you find.

A love letter from when I was on tour in Germany.

A photograph of Ian cooking for me. I loved him once.

NEIL. What's done is done.

SARAH (*reading the laptop screen*). What's this?

NEIL. A fundraiser for Darfur.

They've sent me the menu – fuck knows why.

SARAH (*reads*). Lobster Bisque.

Tray-baked sea bass with crispy bacon and asparagus.

NEIL. Some little hard-nosed producer Elsa Ruane. Can't be more than twelve.

SARAH (*looking at the laptop screen*). Michael Farrell. Dinner for Darfur?

It's kind of obscene.

NEIL. He saw my report in August –

'The UN is piss', says he of the perma smile. 'Let's do something.'

SARAH. Naïve or what?

NEIL. He's got more people interested with one press conference than I did with my 'exclusive' report. When you bring back the facts you foolishly think you'll create political will – instead . . .

SARAH. You just mobilise another celebrity.

NEIL. Why do I bother with this?

SARAH. It's your job. See? It's moved a very visible person to action.

She kisses him. Gets up.

Now my jacket is . . . somewhere.

She moves away.

NEIL. Beg, flatter, bully, hustle – it was the same on the Evening Press twenty years ago. I haven't gotten further – just older.

SARAH (*from off*). Oh come on.

NEIL. Tanya, Jim, public interest, lack of. Now it's back to –

Minister, without introducing drastic change – Ireland will fail to meet its Kyoto obligation. What do you say?

SARAH (*as the Minister*). I'd say that's a whole lot of nasty air, Mr Devlin.

Next question.

NEIL. Exactly. The usual.

Under his breath.

What in under fuck am I doing?

She re-enters with socks and a jacket.

SARAH. What?

NEIL. When are you coming back to me?

SARAH. Depends on how quickly The White Rabbit gets the hang of the Megamix.

He's quite elderly.

NEIL. Oh dear.

SARAH. Ten years ago I was at The Garrick.

Playing in *Juno and the Paycock.*

Now it's 'Mmm mmm tss mmm mmm tss. Alice was her name yo. Get down. Whooo.'

NEIL. Really?

SARAH. No. But nearly.

She puts on her socks.

NEIL. I told you – I can support you.

SARAH. I want to pay my own way. I'm used to it.

Have you seen my . . .

NEIL. Your boots are over there. Could we find a less hazardous place for them?

She puts her boots on. He resumes working.

SARAH. Hey. It's 'The Picture.'

NEIL *looks at her.*

You had another bad dream last night.

NEIL. Didn't realise you were taking on an invalid?

SARAH. Don't say that.

NEIL. I love you.

SARAH. And I love –

NEIL. Darling, let's not parrot it.

SARAH. OK.

NEIL *gets up and helps her on with her jacket.*

NEIL. I'll leave a filthy message on your mobile.

SARAH. I look forward to it.

She kisses him passionately.

Don't forget to eat something.

She exits.

NEIL *goes to a box. He picks up various items.*

SARAH *shouts 'Bye' from off and slams the door.*

NEIL *has found a photograph.*

NEIL (*shouts back*). Bye Zoë . . . ehhh . . .

Maggie . . . ehh . . . Fuck. (*He drops the picture.*) Sarah, Sarah, Sarah.

The drumming gets louder. He leans out of the window.

SHUUUUT IIIIIIIIT. FUUCCKING SHUUUUT IIIIITTTT.

Scene Thirteen

Evening. MAGGIE *is sitting on a park bench. She has a holdall beside her and a guitar.* ALICE (*a bag lady*) *joins her. She is smoking a joint.*

ALICE. If you are looking for business?

MAGGIE. What?

ALICE. If you are looking for business – North-facing is best.

MAGGIE. I am not looking for business.

ALICE. Shove up. That is my seat.

MAGGIE. I don't see your name on it.

ALICE *squashes in beside* MAGGIE.

ALICE. You'll have to learn manners if you are going to hang around the park after hours.

ALICE *pulls deeply on the joint. She offers it to* MAGGIE.
MAGGIE *shakes her head.*

The Boogieman might get you.

MAGGIE. There is no such thing.

ALICE. He catches little girls like you – fucks you and then
keeps you in a cellar.

MAGGIE. The Boogieman isn't real. Neither is Santa Claus or
Hamburglar.

ALICE. Still. You'd want to make a few friends around here.

MAGGIE. I'll be OK.

ALICE. Maybe you shouldn't have run away.

MAGGIE. How do you know?

ALICE. The bag and the tears are a bit of a giveaway.

So what is your story?

Your mother hits you?

MAGGIE. No.

ALICE. Your father drinks?

MAGGIE. No.

ALICE. Your uncle interferes?

MAGGIE. Noo.

ALICE. Oh I get it. You didn't get that pony? Hmm?

Won't give you a mobile phone?

MAGGIE. My dad left my mum for some other woman.

ALICE. Ohhh. Oh that's bad.

MAGGIE. I know.

ALICE. What has she got that your mother hasn't got?

MAGGIE. She's new, I suppose.

ALICE. Congratulations.

You have learned a very important life lesson.

My sister left five kids and a devoted husband for Slavko the coal man.

No, this is true. They had a deaf kid together. Everybody said it was the wrath of God. She worked like a slave so that he could train to be a pilot. Now he flies for Ryanair. Left my poor sister for an airhostess from Leeds with big legs and a ponytail.

Hah? New is better?

MAGGIE *doesn't say anything.*

What about your mother? She's upset?

MAGGIE. She's flipped. Big time.

She met this guy on the internet.

Twenty-five years old and doesn't wear deodorant.

I mean like – I could have scored him.

ALICE. OK. So he's young.

MAGGIE. Calls himself an anarchist cos he once threw a paint bomb at Leinster House.

ALICE. Right. So he's stupid.

MAGGIE. When I was in bed, they slobbered over one another like St Bernards. I could hear stuff.

ALICE. Young, stupid and horny. Good for her.

MAGGIE. We used to be happy. Mum used to laugh.

ALICE. I'm crying here.

She yawns loudly and stretches.

They'll be locking the gates soon.

MAGGIE. Good.

ALICE. You think you can survive the streets?

MAGGIE. I'll be OK.

ALICE. Sure – you can always sell your ass.

MAGGIE. That's gross.

I have my guitar. I can busk.

ALICE. What do you sing?

MAGGIE. Neil Young. Leonard Cohen. My dad used to make me tapes when he went away.

ALICE. Kid, you won't make a penny on Neil Young. You'll end up selling your guitar for twenty euro.

MAGGIE. It's worth two hundred.

ALICE. Desperation effects depreciation.

Pobre bastardita –

MAGGIE. You have no idea.

ALICE. Looking forward to a night out?

A bed in a doorway stinking of piss and vomit – stumbled on by drunks – groped by perverts?

MAGGIE *is quiet.*

Yes, why not?

Punish your parents. Give them a heart attack and when they are dead, you can remember the night you all watched *The Wombles.*

MAGGIE. Before my time, lady.

ALICE. There's a whole wonderland out there.

You can be who you wanna be.

Do what you wanna do.

If you believe that you deserve the crack-whore fucked life that awaits you.

I can hear the park keeper's keys.

Rattle rattle.

What are you going to do?

MAGGIE *gets up.*

MAGGIE. I'd rather go home than have to listen to you.

Goodbye.

ALICE *stretches out on the bench.*

MAGGIE *walks away. She takes out her mobile phone. She dials a number.*

NEIL. This is Neil Devlin. Leave a message or if you have a news story, ring the RTE desk at Extension 2089.

She hangs up.

ALICE. I was a physicist in my country. A physicist, hah?

Scene Fourteen

A rehearsal room. A hip-hop beat in the background.

SARAH *is bathed in sweat – half-dressed in a furry cat costume.*

A WHITE RABBIT *hobbles by.*

SARAH *has got a new message on her mobile. She puts it on loudspeaker.*

IAN (*murderous*). Hi Sarah –

Have you got my Pink Floyd CD? Right.

I know you are busy with your new life.

I have tried to call . . . (*He sighs.*) Thank you.

SARAH. Bugger.

WHITE RABBIT. Is that your chap?

SARAH. Ex-chap, I'm afraid.

WHITE RABBIT. Oh dear oh dear. Did you break his heart?

SARAH. I hope not.

WHITE RABBIT. Oh yes. I'd say you've broken some hearts. You remind me of an actress I worked with in seventy-seven. Lovely girl. What was her name? She's dead now. What was it? It was *The Seagull* and I was playing Medvedenko and she was Masha – I was horribly in love with her. Unfortunately she despised me as much as Masha despises Medvedenko – but then one night . . .

SARAH. Yes?

WHITE RABBIT. Oh dear. I've forgotten.

SARAH. Not to worry.

WHITE RABBIT. Oh dear. I'm forgetting rather a lot these days.

Thank you for coming in with my lines this afternoon.

What was it again?

SARAH. The Queen of Hearts she made some tarts . . .

WHITE RABBIT. All on a summer's day. Yes yes. I remember now.

I will get it.

SARAH. Of course you will.

WHITE RABBIT. It's the little things I can't remember.

But the heat. These costumes. The hip-hop.

SARAH. I think maybe I'll ring Julian.

WHITE RABBIT. Julian informed me he had inserted my scut personally.

I expect that was some sort of smutty joke.

Do you think you might talk to him? That would be good.

SARAH. I'll see you in a bit.

WHITE RABBIT. Please come across the road for a drink.

SARAH. I will.

WHITE RABBIT. The Megamix. That's the one.

I get through by imagining a nice tall G and T.

SARAH. Sounds lovely.

He exits as SARAH *dials*.

WHITE RABBIT. Oh dear. Oh dear. The Knave of Hearts he stole those tarts . . .

SARAH. Hi, is that Julian?

Sarah Rafter? Right? You're on a train to?

Your next show? *Cymbeline*. No, I don't know that one very well. You see, there is a bit of a problem. Hello?

The thing is, I'm running about on stage for ninety minutes in synthetic fur. I'm sweating just putting it on. I can't imagine what it's going to smell like after week two.

No, it's not that I don't like (*the costume*) I love your design.

Hello? Julian?

Not just me. Some of the older members are . . .

Is there any way? Hello?

Hello? Can you hear me?

Scene Fifteen

An office. ELSA *is looking at the tabloids.* REG *is working on a computer.*

The phones are ringing. There is a hum of noise from outside.

REG. Good morning. Born Free Productions.

I'm sorry, she's in a meeting.

I'm afraid we can't give out his number.

ELSA. Oh just fucking hang up.

REG. I'm afraid I can't comment.

The door buzzes.

I'm afraid I don't know.

ELSA (*pressing the intercom button*). No interviews.

REG. I'm afraid.

IAN. But I have an appointment. A photo shoot.

Ian Fenton?

REG. Thank you. Goodbye.

ELSA (*over the intercom*). Don't let anybody else up.

She zaps the door.

IAN. I'll try but it's . . .

There is noise (almost like dogs barking).

Camera clicks. Voices: 'News of the World – any chance of . . . ', 'The Mirror – could I just . . . '

Get off me.

The door slams shut. The noise disappears to a hum.

IAN *enters flustered. He has his camera gear with him.*

Jesus.

ELSA. I know.

IAN. I mean, fucking hell.

ELSA. Have a seat.

IAN. *The Sun* offered money. Another practically bit me.

ELSA goes to a window. Opens it.

The noise again, the camera clicks.

Cries of 'Elsa, Elsa – have you any comment?'

ELSA closes the window.

ELSA. Imagine this – I am lost for words.

REG (*to* IAN). Thank heavens for small mercies.

ELSA. Have you seen the tabloids?

IAN. I'm a broadsheet kind of guy.

ELSA. Have a read.

She throws a paper at him.

REG. Wounded wife says, 'He has shat on me from a great height.'

IAN. Three In A Bed drug-fuelled romp – recipe for disaster.

ELSA (*reads*). 'Elsa Ruane, creator of *The MFCS*, must be furious at celebrity chef Michael Farrell's sordid antics. Allegations of sleaze and drugs look set to pull the curtain on the hip show . . . '

Pause.

IAN. I suppose this means the photo shoot is off?

ELSA. I don't even know where la Farrell is.

Under a stone where the toad belongs probably.

She moves back to the window.

REG *answers the ringing phone.*

REG. Yes. Mmm hmm. / Hmm. She's in a meeting at the moment.

OK. OK.

ELSA. It's a feeding frenzy.

IAN. A fallen idol, every six months, regular as clockwork.

REG. The Clydesdale Bank. They want to withdraw funding from the Chad documentary.

ELSA. They can't have their money back.

Did you remind them it's for the fucking Africans?

Lodge the cheques immediately.

REG. They say they don't want to be associated with sleaze.

ELSA. Get John Burke on the phone.

I'm not having all my projects going down the pan.

Look at this. (*She shows* IAN *a document.*)

The tally for the Darfur benefit. One hundred and seventy-eight thousand, six hundred and fifty-three euro.

REG. Elsa Ruane for John Burke.

ELSA. We're buying a Water Chlorination System for a camp in Chad.

She puts her head in her hands.

Sorry. Sorry.

REG. It's urgent.

ELSA. You will be compensated for today. Don't worry.

IAN. Forget it. (*He gets up to go.*)

You were set up for a fall. Domestic bliss?

Well, it's domestic piss now.

REG. One moment.

ELSA. I'd do it again. Everybody wants a fairytale.

REG. John Burke.

ELSA (*picking up her phone*). John. I understand –

Let's remember who benefits from the funding . . .

What am I going to say to Oxfam? They are expecting . . .

ELSA *looks at* REG. *He opens the window.*

John, John – you were so charming and funny, yes, funny at the Benefit.

Those stories about your MD and his rather large wife. Remind me again why her lip got stuck to the ice bucket?

ELSA *holds out the phone for a moment.*

Hmm? The nation's press are camped outside.

REG *closes the window.*

You will have a think, will you?

Marvellous.

She hangs up.

IAN. It's that easy?

ELSA. Rarely. In this case – raging alcoholic.

IAN *makes to exit.*

IAN. Well – OK then . . .

ELSA. Where are you going?

IAN. Home.

ELSA. Stay. Reg will make tea.

REG. I'm a human being.

ELSA. Not while you're working for me. Please, Reggie.

He gets up reluctantly.

She leans over to IAN.

(*Confidentially.*) I don't want Reg to know but I was having an affair with himself.

IAN. Of course.

O go my man. Well – he's gone.

ELSA. We had an understanding.

IAN. No. He did.

One person in a relationship always knows how it is going to go.

ELSA. He said he loved me.

IAN. We are the humiliated, the shat upon, the deceived.

ELSA. Speak for yourself. I was deceived maybe. Humiliated – never.

IAN. Whatever you say.

ELSA. So she left you.

IAN. She did.

ELSA. You OK?

IAN. Feel nauseous. I'm having revenge fantasies.

I can't eat.

She took the nice towels.

ELSA. You can always buy new towels.

You've got to lick your wounds and move on.

REG *re-enters with milk and sugar.*

IAN. Funny you should say that. I had a dream the other night that I was with Sarah and we were laughing and playing – she was tugging my ears and I was so happy until I realised I was a Red Setter. A fucking Red Setter?

ELSA. There is nothing easy about love.

REG. We coo, we weep, grovel, regress, demand, want, punish, hate.

IAN. Love is your guts on the floor.

ELSA. Love is taking that STD test.

REG. Is that what love is?

ELSA. Where's the tea?

REG. We all knew about you and Michael Farrell.

ELSA. What?

REG. You'd better hope *they* don't find out about it.

They'll tear you to shreds.

ELSA. But I'm only a baby.

IAN. It still doesn't look good.

REG. So what do you say?

The phones start to ring again.

ELSA. I say, keep your face shut and you've got a promotion.

REG. The tea is now off. Not in my job description.

ELSA. I've gotta get an idea.

REG. No more swilling about in despair.

ELSA. I've got to do something.

IAN. Do something. Sometimes it's better to admit defeat.

ELSA. Ian. You're not talking my language.

And I'm hoping to take you home tonight.

IAN. Oh?

REG. That's the best offer you are going to get.

ELSA. You should make something out of your revenge fantasies.

If I was an artist, that's what I'd do.

REG. Revenge is a whetstone. Sharpen up.

IAN. I'm not an artist.

REG. Since when did that stop anyone?

IAN. It's funny but . . .

ELSA. Yes?

IAN. My father used to take pictures of my mother to wind her up.

June angry chopping carrots. 1976.

June raging over ill-judged comment about weight. 1977.

June slams the yellow front door, 1978, won him a Kodak prize.

And it got me thinking . . .

ELSA. That's hardcore. There's something in that . . .

There is a crashing noise.

REG *looks out the window.*

REG. If we don't feed them, we may be in big trouble.

IAN. What's the worst they can do?

REG. Print the truth.

ELSA. Feed them?

Fuck it – yes.

I think it's about time Africa gave something back.

IAN. I'm not quite with you.

ELSA. Of course I'm saddened by what's alleged about Michael Farrell. I hope he manages to overcome his problems.

REG. What? Like he can't zip it?

ELSA. But I'm more upset that it's deflecting media interest from a humanitarian crisis which has been called 'the worst in the world.'

I'd like to talk to you about that.

REG. Give her an Oscar.

ELSA. Here we go, boys. Mother Elsa fucking Peron.

IAN. What do I know?

ELSA *goes to the window.*

ELSA. Watch me.

She opens the window.

The noise rises.

Scene Sixteen

Dressing room.

ZOË *is waiting.*

A musical version of Alice in Wonderland *is heard over the tannoy.*

Various lines are spoken – we hear SARAH *singing/rapping.*

THE QUEEN OF HEARTS. Behead her, suppress her – off with her head.

SARAH.
    And she said
    Off with her head.
    But Alice wasn't dead.
    She was cool she was cheeky.
    It was damn near freaky.
    Cos she is
    Alice in Wonder.
    Alice in Wonder.
    Alice.
    In.
    WONDERLANNNNNND.

    Check it out.

Applause. The play continues over the tannoy. After a moment or two, SARAH *runs in. She is wearing a furry cat costume – with a large white tail, whiskers and cat ears.*

She has a huge clown like smile painted on and is sweating profusely. She is the Cheshire Cat.

SARAH (*humming to herself*).
    Alice in Wonder, Alice in Wonder.

SARAH *sees* ZOË.

Oh. You gave me a fright.

ZOË. Nothing to the fright you gave me.

SARAH. What?

ZOË. I'm Neil Devlin's wife. Zoë.

Pause.

SARAH. Oh? Oh.

ZOË. I Googled you.

The internet is a wonderful thing.

And then I found myself passing by.

Nice flowers. Did my husband give them to you?

SARAH. Yes. Yes he did.

How did you get in here?

ZOË. The stage door was open. Nobody was around.

I was about to leave when I saw a photograph of Neil on
your mirror. Do you know where it was taken?

SARAH. No I don't.

ZOË. It was taken on a family trip to Prague two years ago.

We so rarely go away as a family.

Our daughter took it. It's good, isn't it?

SARAH. Yes.

ZOË. That is typical of Neil –

Typical he should give you that photograph. He's such a shit.

SARAH. There's a coffee shop across the road.

I can meet you there in twenty minutes.

ZOË. No.

SARAH. What do you mean, 'No'?

ZOË. I don't mind waiting.

SARAH. I'm on stage in five minutes.

ZOË. I don't really want to go.

SARAH. Look – this is between you and Neil. Leave me out
of it.

ZOË. I can't.

SARAH. What do you want from me?

ZOË. Sometime ago I might have said my husband.

But recently I've been having fantasies à la Bobbit.

She wasn't found guilty, you know.

Temporary insanity was blamed.

SARAH. Are you trying to frighten me? Is that why you are here?

ZOË. I'm here because I want to see the woman my husband left me for.

Turns out it's the Cheshire Cat.

SARAH. I don't want this. Just leave, please.

ZOË breaks down.

ZOË. I shouldn't have come.

SARAH. Are you all right?

ZOË. No. (*She sits.*) I'm finding it difficult to . . . I'll be OK . . . in a minute. Sorry.

The QUEEN OF HEARTS *flounces in. She is wearing a tall spiky crown – a red velvet robe slashed to the middle.*

THE QUEEN. Night after fucking night. You know?

That little amateur gives me nothing.

I'm singing my tits off and she's staring at the Nine of Spades. I mean, where in *Alice in* fucking *Wonderland* does it say that Alice has the hots for the Nine of Spades? The kids must notice something. Those two should get a fucking room. Oh yeah and on my biggest laugh – 'What's happened to my bush?'– do you know what Alice was doing? Complete focus-pulling.

Fucking Am Dram or what? Yeah and the White Rabbit is about to drop dead any . . . Oh.

SARAH. This is Zoë.

ZOË. I'm sorry, excuse me. I'm leaving.

THE QUEEN. Stay where you are. Welcome welcome.

Are you all right, Zoë?

ZOË. Yes.

THE QUEEN. No you are not. What's happened?

SARAH. It's nothing. Private.

ZOË. My husband.

THE QUEEN. Oh. (*She looks to* SARAH, *back to* ZOË.) Oh . . .
Poor poor Zoë.

Poor you. Another woman?

ZOË. Yes.

THE QUEEN *comforts* ZOË.

THE QUEEN. I mean us gals should stick together. Don't you
think, Sarah?

SARAH. Mmm hmm.

THE QUEEN. Those types that go with married men –

A nice dinner and the Sisterhood's up in flames like the
fucking Sambuca.

She's better off without him, isn't she?

SARAH. Yep.

ZOË. It's hard. When it's over.

THE QUEEN. You think you're getting UHT but it fucking
curdles all the same.

SARAH. People don't belong to people.

ZOË. Yes they do.

THE QUEEN. Word of advice? Keep men on a very short
leash.

You've got to cattle prod them with one of those electric
things when they get a bit frisky.

They don't understand niceness. They understand pain.

ZOË. My daughter too.

THE QUEEN. Taking it badly?

ZOË. She's tried to run away. We had a row.

I think she's ashamed of me.

THE QUEEN. Oh poor Zoë, poor poor Zoë.

Of course she's not. (*Hissing to* SARAH.) Tissues.

SARAH *hands* ZOË *a handful of Kleenex.*

ZOË. I feel so stupid.

THE QUEEN. Nothing to feel stupid about.

It's frightening not to be loved, isn't it? Makes one feel like a child again. Hmm?

ZOË. Mmm hmm.

TANNOY. Miss Evans to the stage, please. Two minutes.

THE QUEEN. If you could get this woman's number you could put it up around town in telephone boxes. You know – the escort-agency gag. Wouldn't that be fun? Go on – unleash the childish impulse to destroy.

ZOË *nods.*

SARAH. Hilarious.

THE QUEEN *grabs a cigarette and stuffs it in her mouth. She flounces out the door.*

THE QUEEN. Magic of the musicals and all that.

Sarah – Let's knock five minutes off – I'm bored outta my shite with this half.

Hey Zoë?

ZOË. Yes?

THE QUEEN. Off with her head.

ZOË. Thank you. Thank you very much.

She exits.

ZOË *dries her tears.*

The Queen of Hearts is lovely.

SARAH. Look. I have to go on in a minute.

ZOË. I didn't want this.

This is not the life I wanted.

Having to start all over again. And I find it difficult to
contemplate sex without love . . . but I've been – how shall
I say – experimenting with my newly liberated self. And last
night I ended up getting absolutely rat-arsed at a publishing
do and I begged the writer du jour to have sex with me.
I mean begged him. I was not at all attracted to this guy but
somehow my mouth was saying things and I was telling
him I was going to send him to outer space and back –
so the next thing he's decided we're going to Belfast for
the night. Well, we get as far as Dungannon, have an
excruciating fuck in the front seat of his car, yes, front seat,
I kid you not. Then he turned the car around – drove
without speaking and dropped me off on O'Connell Bridge.
It was like I was a teenager again. You see, it seems to me
I attract shit fucks –

Or fuck shits.

What is it about me?

SARAH. I can't help you. I don't know what to say.

ZOË. My daughter is fifteen going on thirty-five.

Does Neil talk about her?

SARAH. Of course.

ZOË. She wants to be a singer.

Fame ostensibly is a viable career in her world.

SARAH *hesitates.*

You have no children. I have responsibilities.

SARAH. I'm telling you – talk to Neil.

ZOË. Ian is rather a nice chap if I recall. I don't normally go to
openings – but the Spar idea intrigued me. Funnily enough
I remember you – even through the fur. Tight little T-shirt
and low-slung jeans. Men like the obvious. God, it's
depressing.

SARAH. You should go.

ZOË. O come on, come on. Don't be shy. We're just talking.

SARAH. I'm working.

ZOË. Who approached who?

TANNOY. Miss Rafter.

Mr Duggan.

Miss Scully.

Mr McElroy.

Stand by for the Wonderland Megamix.

SARAH *tries to get past.*

SARAH. Excuse me.

ZOË. Not until you tell me.

Pause.

SARAH. Neil approached me.

ZOË. How? What did he say?

SARAH. I can't remember.

ZOË. Of course you do. You probably re-ran it many times.

It's what people do.

SARAH. Please don't ask me.

ZOË. I won't let you past till I know.

SARAH. He told me I smelled great.

ZOË. He told you that.

SARAH. You asked. I'm sorry.

ZOË. He obviously hasn't met you after the matinee performance.

SARAH. There is a problem with the suit. I . . .

ZOË. Then?

SARAH. Then he asked to see me again.

TANNOY. Two minutes to the Megamix.

Miss Rafter to the stage immediately.

ZOË. How often?

SARAH. Whenever we could. Once a month. Once every three months, three times a week. Whenever. Please.

ZOË. I see. You were his conferences, his last-minute interviews, late drinks / with friends –

SARAH. I feel sorry for all that's happened.

ZOË. No you don't. You're glad.

And Neil continues on like a headless chicken.

You think you know him after only guessing?

SARAH. Let me by.

ZOË. He was finished when I met him. Booted from the Beeb for drinking and erratic behaviour. I turned him around. I saved him.

SARAH. You can't save a person.

TANNOY. Sarah, Sarah to the stage.

ZOË *blocks* SARAH*'s way to the exit.*

ZOË. And what kind of life is this?

If the escalator ain't moving at thirty-five it ain't never gonna move. What does he see in you?

SARAH. I don't know what he sees in me but he makes me feel hopeful.

ZOË. There we are.

We're all of us looking for a lifeline.

TANNOY. Sarah, get off the toilet.

SARAH. Goodbye Zoë.

ZOË *stops her.*

ZOË. I know what he sees in you. There's a kind of blankness.

Nothing sticks. I presume he finds that a comfort.

SARAH. Get out of my way.

ZOË. Let's see how hopeful this makes you feel.

ZOË *exits, slamming the door.*

SARAH *tries to exit but the door is locked or* ZOË *is holding it shut.*

SARAH. What are you doing? Open the door.

TANNOY. Sarah – for fuck's sake – Alice is kakking her pants out there – move it.

ZOË (*shouts*). What happens if you never recover?

SARAH. Zoë, please open this door. HELP. HELP.

TANNOY. Sarah, Jesus Christ, Sarah, you fucking dingbat.

Go Megamix, go.

The Megamix blasts across the tannoy.

Scene Seventeen

Outside the station.

JIM *strides along, pulling deeply on a cigarette.*

NEIL *has been trying to catch up with him.*

NEIL. Jim? Jim?

JIM *turns around.*

JIM. Yes?

Fucking Jaysus, can I not have a smoke?

NEIL. You're supposed to be off them.

JIM. Don't tell Carol.

NEIL. Carol's not too fond of me at the moment.

JIM. Ah yes. She's in the Zoë camp. Not to worry.

You still have some friends left.

NEIL. Have you looked at my pitch?

JIM. Think, think – remind me again. Darfur?

NEIL. Women and children have been trying to return to Abu Gamra –

JIM. This is your fucking village – yeah?

NEIL. Yes. The special we made in August?

JIM. So remind me – the new hook?

NEIL. I want to go back to the site of the massacre –

JIM. Nahh.

NEIL. – and interview these Zaghawa women who I understand have been trying to return home.

JIM. What's new in that?

NEIL. One woman's father was beheaded in front of her, another's baby – thrown into a burning hut. Another woman and her eight-year-old daughter Kalima were gang raped by the Janjaweed. They've lost their homes, their village has been razed to the ground but they're still trying. These women are trying to make a new life in all this extraordinary hatred and suffering.

JIM. You know what it's like. The situation is ongoing.

The public are no longer interested.

How's your little one taking you and . . . ?

NEIL. Not so little. Maggie. She's fifteen.

JIM. Course. Same age as Tommy. They turn into right little shites, don't they, hah?

If only he could string two words together –

(*He winces in pain and rubs his stomach.*) Ahhhh.

NEIL. Jim – we filmed the dead. It would be good to find the living.

JIM *takes out a box of red Rennie from his jacket pocket – pops a few and crunches loudly.*

JIM. They make you shit concrete. Like delivering a fucking coke tin out your arse.

He stubs out his cigarette.

NEIL. Are you listening to me at all? Or am I wasting my fucking time?

JIM *pops some more Rennie and crunches.*

JIM. Ah now. Don't be like that.

NEIL. Sorry. Sorry.

JIM. Thing is . . . I quite like the idea – you get me?

NEIL. Great.

JIM. But the timing is shite. The bill for the fucking incinerator in Meath is being debated on the third –

Then it's Environment week – you'll be up and down the country like a hoor's knickers – spinning plates.

NEIL. I can move the dates to the end of the month. That's not a problem.

JIM. Neil – we don't have the budget.

NEIL. I'll travel third class in some bucket carrier. There are no feeds.

I'll even go robohack. Operation / will be half the cost.

JIM. OK. OK, Neil.

I have four words to say on the subject of you and Darfur.

NEIL. Yes?

JIM. Get fucking over it.

NEIL. Sorry?

JIM. I'm aware you have been lobbying to get back but the station does not have the resources to monitor, review. Plus, at the end of the day, when all is said and done, the heel of the hunt –

NEIL. What?

JIM. It's old fucking news.

Neil. Old fucking news whatever – I think the station has a moral responsibility to follow up. – slow-motion genocide – two years. I really need to / get back out there.

JIM. That is the point. *Your need* is not newsworthy.

It's not going to feed the fucking beast.

NEIL. I can't let it be just another story.

JIM. Ahhhhh. (*He rubs his stomach.*)

Fuck's sake. Are you drinking again?

NEIL. I've been dry for years.

JIM. Is this something to do with Zoë and yourself? You could have some time off.

He crunches some more Rennie.

NEIL. I don't need time off. Maybe you do.

JIM. I keep telling Carol she's giving me acid.

Puts those cherry tomatoes on everything.

They're good for the, you know . . .

NEIL. Prostate.

JIM. Right, yeah, so prove it, I say to her. She's fucking killing me.

NEIL. How long have you known me?

JIM. I was at your wedding. I sang 'Born to be Wild' with your wife's father.

NEIL. Right. Can't you even help me out here?

JIM. Tanya Sullivan's one of the top producers here.

She didn't get to make her programme because her man in Darfur didn't turn up for the filming. He was too busy doing his own thing. You get me?

NEIL. Is she still going on about it?

JIM. You're too old to be acting the cunt. It's not attractive any more.

People are talking.

NEIL. Fuck them.

JIM. Tanya's got a green light to make a programme in Chad. A co-production with Born Free Productions. Pilgrimage with a Water Chlorination System.

Elsa Ruane. You know her?

NEIL. Yeah. Ambitious little minx.

JIM. Mentioned your name as a replacement presenter for Farrell.

Tanya overruled it. Would have got you out there with a decent crew.

He takes out a cigarette – prepares to light it.

NEIL. It's the fags.

JIM. Hah?

NEIL. They are causing the acid.

JIM. Yeah, yeah, I fucking know it. I've got to have a little pleasure now that Carol's gone off the you-know-what.

He lights up and draws deeply.

Now listen to me.

I told Tanya your marriage break-up may have been 'difficult'.

NEIL. What?

JIM. She was sympathetic. Been having an affair with the DPP.

Desperate for him to leave his wife.

An amount of arse-licking and a guarantee of limited maverick behaviour perhaps? It might be your way out there –

NEIL. You talked to her for me?

JIM. You still have some friends, Neil.

Now. Hostile-environment training has to be your next port of call.

NEIL. Longmoor?

JIM. That's it. Tanya insists you do the course.

No more UN escorts.

NEIL. Jesus – Jim. We got stuck outside curfew.

JIM. As my lad Tommy might say – 'Whatever.'

You haven't done a risk-assessment course in four years.

Pause.

Take it or fucking leave it.

NEIL. OK. OK. I'll do it.

JIM. In the meantime.

Prepare to lick some ass. Ho ho.

Jaysus. (*He eats some more Rennie.*)

Scene Eighteen

A darkened hospital ward. ALICE is lying on a bed with wheels.

The sound of a life-support machine pips away.

SARAH as Doctor O'Toole strides by.

ALICE (*croaks*). Doctor O'Toole.

SARAH stops and enters.

SARAH. Alice. How are you?

ALICE. Not good, Doctor.

I'm going to die – aren't I?

SARAH. We are all going to die – you just have a better idea when than most.

ALICE (*getting upset*). Oh Doctor.

SARAH takes her hand.

How long have I got?

SARAH. Maybe a week, a month, could even be as long as a year.

It's up to you.

ALICE. What do you mean, Doctor?

SARAH. It's up to you how you deal with it.

You can decide to fight this.

ALICE. But I just feel so tired. I have no fight left in me.

I have such pain.

SARAH *picks up* ALICE*'s chart and peruses it.*

SARAH. Pain. My God. I was holding my baby sister when I
was told of the death of my grandfather. I dropped the poor
child.

The flat line suddenly – beeeeeeeeep.

ALICE *dies.* SARAH *drops the chart.*

No . . . Noooooo.

From off, FREDDY *the floor manager shouts.*

FREDDY. And cut. Let's have a look at that.

A bell rings. The sound of tape rewinding.

NEIL *has entered. He has a travel bag with him.*

NEIL. Hello Doctor / O'Toole.

SARAH. Were you watching?

NEIL. I sneaked in as the red light went on. You were
wonderful.

SARAH. Don't take the piss.

NEIL. Would I?

Doctor O'Toole has millions in her grasp.

SARAH. One point two million. Yes. / You should be so lucky.

NEIL. If I had that kind of exposure I'd be –

SARAH. Jon Snow.

NEIL. Right.

SARAH *reaches out to touch* NEIL.

SARAH. You're sweating.

NEIL. I'm fine. But I'm on the run.

FREDDY. Final checks. / We're going to do a close-up of the
chart falling.

SARAH. Wait for me.

She steps back into place.

FREDDY. Turning? / 5–4–3–2–1 and action.

SARAH *drops the chart.*

Camera still rolling.

Sarah, can you angle the chart to camera one – so we can see what's on it?

That's it.

Action.

SARAH *drops the chart again.*

Check that.

SARAH *steps out.*

NEIL. Are you finished soon?

SARAH. First I have to rid the hospital of MRSA.

NEIL. Impressive.

SARAH. Then after lunch, an ethical crisis. Kiss or Catheter?

FREDDY. Sarah, can I have you back in position for one line?

He spots NEIL.

Look it here. If it isn't the great man himself.

So is it Kerry or Kabul, this weather, hah?

NEIL. Just keeping my head down.

FREDDY *listens to something on his headset.*

FREDDY. 'Pain. My God', etc.

They're saying upstairs grandfather sounds like granfarter.

NEIL *wipes the sweat off his face.*

C'mere, Neil, hi. Would ya think of coming over to our side?

SARAH *steps back into position.*

Sure, at the end of the day it's all drama, hah?

SARAH. Is something up?

FREDDY. OK. Going for the one line. Turning?

NEIL. I have to fucking travel.

SARAH. Where?

NEIL. London.

FREDDY. 5–4–3–2–1 action.

SARAH. Pain. My God. I was holding my baby sister when I
was told of the death of my grandfather. I dropped the poor
child.

FREDDY. And cut. / Check that.

SARAH *steps out.*

SARAH. London?

NEIL. A course. Mandatory before I go to Africa.

SARAH. You're going?

FREDDY. Good work.

That's clear everybody.

The bell rings. The lights go up.

NEIL. I'm going to Chad but if I get a visa, I'll get to Darfur.

ALICE *is wheeled off along with all the medical apparatus.*

ALICE. Oh thank you. It was wonderful working / with you.
I played Arkadina for twenty years at the Warsaw . . .

SARAH. Oh yes and you. Thank you.

FREDDY. That's a studio move for cast and crew / – so Studio
B for the MRSA scene.

The stage is empty by the end of FREDDY*'s instructions –*
SARAH *is left alone with* NEIL.

SARAH. You got what you wanted?

NEIL. Just about. If I get to make my programme.

SARAH. That's good.

NEIL. Good, yeah.

SARAH. Will it be over then?

NEIL. What?

SARAH. Three a.m. this morning. You interviewed the wardrobe.

Your eyes wild in your head.

NEIL. Was I good?

SARAH. Then you screamed when you saw your reflection.

What are you seeing?

NEIL. It's not always horrors.

SARAH. Tell me.

NEIL. What's to tell?

Sometimes it's a small thing – a child holding a dead parent's shoe.

SARAH. Was it like this with Zoë?

Is this how it goes? Just tell me.

NEIL. The last trip was hard.

SARAH. I know. But something is different.

NEIL. What?

SARAH. I'm no longer the object of your obsession.

NEIL. I've been preoccupied. I know.

SARAH. I'm beginning to suspect that you always are.

NEIL. My conscience is a dimly lit cellar.

But know that I love you.

SARAH. What can I do?

NEIL. Do? You've saved me.

SARAH. Leave salvation to Jesus and co. I'd like a functioning boyfriend.

NEIL. At least you've got Doctor O'Toole.

SARAH. When I was at drama school I said

I'd rather cut my legs off than be in something like this.

Throw art to the dogs – I'd rather be working.

Anyway, we need a washing machine.

NEIL. Don't knock it.

SARAH. I'm not really.

I've wasted too many years.

Waiting – waiting to be defined by this job.

Knocked by the no's.

Grateful for the yes's.

Living the life of a desperado.

Feels a bit silly past thirty but this is how it goes for me.

NEIL. It's no job for a grown-up.

SARAH. We have more in common than you think.

We've both been postponing life.

You've had a front seat at other people's conflicts.

Time to face your own.

FREDDY *calls for* SARAH.

FREDDY. Sarah? Make-up checks, please.

NEIL. You've been doing a lot of thinking.

SARAH. It's not beyond me.

Call me when you land. I worry.

NEIL. Every evening. OK?

SARAH. And for God's sake eat?

NEIL. You're a wonderful woman, Doctor O'Toole.

I'll walk you to your next scene.

He takes her hand.

Scene Nineteen

Hostile-Environment training.

Darkness. The rev of a Land Rover engine. Car lights.

NEIL *is pushed onto stage. His hands are tied behind his back. He is out of breath.*

A MAN *in a headscarf has a Kalashnikov.*

The Land Rover is revved to a deafening pitch and the MAN *fires a number of rounds. He roars in Arabic.*

MAN. On your knees.

NEIL. Jesus. Yes. I . . . I . . . I . . . I . . . I . . . I knee . . . yes, kneel.

Oh . . . Please . . . I . . . just . . . ah uh I . . .

MAN. You want I shoot?

NEIL. OK. OK. OK. OK. Please. Please . . .

I'm kneeling.

I have.

A daughter –

A photograph . . . in my wallet . . . please I . . .

Do you have children?

MAN. They were killed in the war.

NEIL. I'm so sorry. So very sorry . . .

MAN. So am I. There have been many tears in my country.

We have been shaken up and down like a salt cellar.

NEIL. Oh God.

MAN. You have a God?

NEIL. Yes. I'm Irish you see. Irish?

MAN. I know Ireland.

NEIL. Devout. It's a devout country. We didn't want war.

We . . . we . . .

We believe in forgiveness . . . I . . . I . . . mercy . . . we . . . we . . .

MAN. Look me in the eye.

Who did the children offend that we should cry for mercy?

NEIL. I am – beg.

I am begging you.

MAN. There was no mercy for my lovely girls.

When the bombs came.

NEIL. We're a neutral country.

We marched in opposition to the war.

We too have been colonised, divided by religion.

MAN. What does your Ireland's 'neutrality' mean?

NEIL. We do not take part in any side of a conflict.

MAN. Explain to me then why the US military aircraft landed in Shannon for refuelling purposes?

NEIL. The government's position was totally at variance with the views of the Irish people. Our neutrality has been contravened.

MAN (*pulls down his scarf*). For fuck sake, Paddy, you have a military policy of non-alignment but it's not enshrined constitutionally.

NEIL. These guys aren't going to know that.

MAN. Don't be so sure. (*He pulls his scarf back up.*)

The planes that landed may be the planes that killed my children.

Your government is guilty as fuck.

He puts the gun (or machete) to NEIL*'s head.*

There is blood on all your hands.

NEIL. I have a daughter. Maggie. She needs me . . . Want to.

MAN. Should have thought of that before you came out here then.

So say your prayers. In Irish.

NEIL. Yes. Yes, I . . . I hope I can remember –

MAN. Pray.

NEIL. Ar n-Athair, ata ar neamh. Go naoimher d'aimn. Go dtaghta da riacht go n-eanter do thoill ar an talamh.

MAN. It sounds like you are spitting nails.

NEIL. So does Arabic . . . I mean I find . . . Don't you?

That's what's good about it. The similarities?

MAN. Don't ever ask questions, Paddy. Don't try to be funny.

NEIL. Sorry. Sorry.

MAN. You think your God will save you? Maybe Delta Forces will chopper in and defeat me?

NEIL. My fate is in your hands.

MAN. Your fate is in God's hands. But you have no God.

NEIL. Fuck.

MAN. Roy Keane.

NEIL. What? I mean yes. Yes. Roy Keane. Footie. Irish.

MAN. Saipan. What a disaster.

NEIL. Yes. Yes. Yes. Yes. Yes. Saipan. World Cup. A disaster. My God . . . a disaster.

MAN. How could he do that? To betray his country?

NEIL. Well. There are many schools of thought on that.

But one says . . .

MAN. There is no excuse.

NEIL. No, of course.

MAN. Oh yes. I am footie fan. Oh yes.

Manchester United, heh.

He laughs.

NEIL. I'm a fan too. I've been a fan since I was a kid.

There was a fan club in the East End of the town. My father brought me on Saturday mornings. My God. What a coincidence. To come all this way and meet another . . .

MAN. I'm an Arsenal fan.

Turn around, Infidel.

NEIL. Shit.

The MAN unties NEIL's hands.

The MAN *takes his own scarf and cloak off, revealing a British Army uniform.*

MAN. You didn't do so good, son. You talked about your family too early. That's an ace card. Don't throw it away.

So remember –

Don't panic.

Control your breathing.

Make eye contact.

And whatever you do – don't ask fucking questions.

NEIL. Yeah. Right.

MAN. Had you going there.

NEIL. You were very convincing.

MAN. Didn't expect the kidnapping, did you, Paddy?

NEIL. Not at five o'clock in the morning.

MAN. It's a reality for you lot now.

I know Ireland well. Served three tours.

The Bogside, Ballymurphy. Fucking terrible times.

Direland, we used to call it. Fucking Dire – land.

Things have changed now. Peace Process, Celtic Tiger and what-have-you.

NEIL. We've come a long way.

MAN. Where are you for next?

NEIL. Chad and then Darfur – if I can get a visa.

MAN. Ah yes . . . the same war. Over and over.

Rwanda, Srebrenicia, Darfur – Each needless death diminishes us all.

Every man is a piece of the continent.

I get tired sometimes.

NEIL. I've left a wife. My daughter.

MAN. Join the club. I'm on my third marriage.

NEIL. Sometimes I forget I have a family.

NEIL *puts his head in his hands.*

MAN. Takes its toll.

NEIL. I saw the massacre – I was there and yet I've missed the breakdown of my own relationship. I felt more for a woman I'd been having an affair with than I did for my wife.

MAN. Take a deep breath. See, when you do these courses you tend to think it's a piece of piss.

But you've been hearing about massive blood loss, legs flying a hundred feet in the air, minefields, nerve-gas agents. Frankly if you're not fucking depressed at this stage . . .

NEIL. I don't know if I can keep going. (*He starts to tremble.*)

NEIL *starts to cry.*

MAN. Son?

NEIL. Kewa roota.

MAN. Are you there, son?

Come back. Come back to us. Can you hear me?

NEIL *is shaking.*

NEIL. Yeah yeah.

MAN. Tell me about the new woman. Lad? Come on.

NEIL. She's . . .

MAN. She's what?

NEIL. She's . . . new.

MAN. Very good.

NEIL. I don't know. I don't know. I love her.

MAN. I'll treat you to a rendition of 'What I Did For Love' later.

That's pretty fucking mind-altering and all.

Thing is, love never saved anyone but it's the best distraction we get.

NEIL. It's the main item on the menu.

MAN. In that case, you've got a bit of an about turn to do, son.

NEIL. I don't know. I don't know.

MAN. Don't bother making any sense of it. Just do what you can.

Pause.

I realised that in Northern Ireland when I saw a child's entrails on a blackened pavement.

There's no sense in anything.

Pause.

Some of you lot are cooked and don't even know it.

NEIL. I can't be cooked. The good ones were famous at my age – or had made a difference.

MAN. Glory and excitement. The Holy Grail.

NEIL. I'll be fine.

MAN. No, you won't. You're cracking. You've cracked.

You'll make a show of yourself on the plane – when you go out in the field. Somewhere. Darfur doesn't need you. You need it to detour.

NEIL. From what?

MAN. Your own story – the one you can't predict.

Your own story – (of which you'll never know the outcome).

The MAN *walks away. He throws his jacket to* NEIL.

It will be rain tonight.

He exits.

NEIL. What? You're just leaving me?

The Land Rover starts up.

MAN (*shouting back*). It's part of the course.

He revs the engine.

Don't forget – you're getting gassed in an hour.

Scene Twenty

An area off the main gallery.

Two large posters of IAN's *exhibition hang from the ceiling.*

A photograph of SARAH *and of* IAN. EVIDENCE *is stamped on the front of both.*

ELSA *looks into the lens of a TV camera. She fixes her hair and rubs lipstick off her teeth.*

ELSA. We're coming to you from The Green Lane Gallery for the opening of 'Evidence' – the new exhibition by photographer Ian Fenton. It's a forensic and often brutal examination of the dying days of a real-life relationship. Art or revenge? Photography or home snaps?

Or finger on the pulse of our insatiable appetite for all things 'Reality'? We're going to talk to some of the visitors and have a look.

ALICE *enters, sweeping and dusting.*

Excuse me? Could I just ask?

ALICE. I just work here.

She continues to sweep.

ELSA. That's OK.

Have you had a look at the exhibition?

ALICE. I have.

She continues to sweep.

ELSA. Would you mind telling us what you think?

ALICE. Do you really want my opinion?

ELSA. Yes, I really do.

ALICE. The only thing he didn't put in, was his arsehole.

This guy, this Ian – this boo-hoo cry baby.

He should, as they say, 'Get a life.'

She dumped him, found someone else. That's it. Kaput.

Make an exhibition out of it?

Making an exhibition out of himself more like.

ELSA. It's a small story of pain, yes, but isn't that what we obsess about?

We think we look outwards but when it comes down to it, it's Me, Myself And I.

ALICE. Phhhhhuuuuhh. People these days. Whinge, cringe, moan, cry.

Ohh I have stress – I need a holiday.

Ahh I'm not having enough orgasms – better see a therapist.

Oooh I'll never be famous – get on Reality TV.

Countries burning and bleeding and nobody cares.

And you really think anybody is gonna care cos this loser got dumped?

She sweeps her way out.

Have a good day.

ELSA. Thank you for that, Mrs . . . ? (*But* ALICE *has gone.*)

Well, strong words there from a member of the public.

I'm going to take a look myself.

And I'll let you know if this is a triumph or a triumph of marketing over matter.

ELSA *nods to camera to signal the end of that tape run.*

OK. Let's move. Reg? You know – we might just edit some of that out.

They exit and cross paths with ZOË *whose mobile phone is ringing.*

She looks younger and more colourful.

ZOË. Hi. Hi, I'm at an exhibition.

Just found a quiet corner.

What are you doing?

ZOË *listens then laughs dirtily.*

Stop it, you naughty boy.

I can't talk. I can't talk. I can't. OK, OK.

Who am I now? (*She barks discreetly into the phone.*)
That's right, I am Mistress Bitch and Mistress Bitch wants
you.

IAN *enters during the call.*

IAN. Sorry. Zoë? Is Maggie about?

ZOË (*becoming businesslike*). I'll call you back.

Thank you for that.

Yep. Bye.

She hangs up.

Hello.

The catalogue's arrived all right?

IAN. You did a great job.

ZOË. It's your work. Your words. I just print it.

IAN. You look good. No. Great.

ZOË. I've been mainlining St John's Wort for some months.
It's really quite amazing.

IAN. Pain is a four-letter word but you don't die from it.

ZOË. I like that. Yeah.

I'm moving on. Moved on.

IAN. I'm really delighted, Zoë.

ZOË. And thank you for putting Maggie in touch with Elsa
Ruane.

The gig here. The slot on *The Afternoon Show*. She is so
excited.

IAN. Elsa thinks she got something. And if Elsa thinks that . . .
well . . .

ELSA *enters with her cameraman,* REG.

ELSA. Quite a few crits out there. It's going to be hardcore.

IAN. Not even thinking about it.

ELSA. Is Maggie about? It's nearly time.

ZOË. Putting the finishing touches to her new look.

I'll wrestle her from the mirror. (*She moves to exit.*)

And Ian?

It's a great stitch-up job.

IAN. That's not quite what I had in mind.

ZOË *exits.*

IAN *looks after her.*

ELSA. Sorry, Ian? Ian?

IAN. I don't know if this was such a good idea.

ELSA. Yeah. Ian?

IAN. What?

ELSA. Too late.

I need to record an interview.

IAN. I feel a bit sick.

ELSA. Less of the 'revisiting sites of pain'. That's so last decade.

A few gags. Hmm?

IAN. Who am I? Max Bygraves?

ELSA. Oh shut up. Come on. Look handsome.

IAN. I'm trying.

SARAH *enters.*

ELSA. Are we set?

REG. Rolling.

IAN. This exhibition . . . is about . . . setting the past down squarely where it is visible. There is a danger . . . in ignoring it . . . or in believing we leave our past behind us . . . in some virtual Left / Luggage.

SARAH. You complete asshole.

IAN. Hello Sarah. How are you? / This is Elsa.

SARAH. Fucking vulturism. Hack at the rotting corpse of what was us.

ELSA (*to* REG). Keep the cameras rolling.

SARAH. You photographed the sheets after the last time we made love? How did you know it was the last time?

IAN. Call it artistic licence.

SARAH. Pictures of me in my underwear? On the toilet?

Pictures of the dirty knives I incorrectly used?

What kind of sick pathetic sadso are you?

IAN. Are you hurt?

SARAH. Hurt, disturbed, mortified.

Are you glad?

IAN. Your leaving me is the most painful incident of my life. /

Why would I be glad?

SARAH. Is it? The most painful incident? / I don't believe that.

IAN. I think I've recycled it well.

SARAH (*pointing to the overhead poster*). And that's my photograph. I took it of you that day / in the bedroom.

IAN. Prove it.

SARAH. You twisted bastard.

IAN. I don't have to listen to this. /

You're not my girlfriend any more.

SARAH. Well, listen to this – You don't have permission / to expose me like this.

IAN. I don't need your permission.

SARAH. Anybody that knows us knows that's me. Even if they don't know us. I'm recognisable in the pictures. You are cashing in on my fame –

IAN. Don't be ridiculous. There is not one close-up picture of you.

SARAH. I have a strong case for legal action.

REG. You'd be surprised.

ELSA. No one owns the copyright to their own life story.

SARAH. Who are you?

ELSA. I'm the producer of this show.

SARAH. Oh fuck off, you tart. I know you shagged him while we were still together.

ELSA. There's no need to be vulgar.

SARAH. Let's see if you are saying that when I sue the arse off you.

ELSA. I'm also a friend of Neil's. Didn't he tell you?

Dinner for Darfur. / It's changed my life.

SARAH. What?

IAN. It's a small but cosy world.

SARAH. This is unbelievable. Are you filming?

ELSA. One euro from every catalogue sold tonight goes to our Save Darfur campaign.

SARAH. What exactly will five euro do?

IAN. Sarah. Ow.

REG. Every little helps.

ELSA. We're doing something, Sarah. Don't you believe in / doing something?

SARAH. Hang on – you're saying that – to the camera.

ELSA. I'm making a documentary. / It's what I do.

SARAH. You have no permission to use anything on that tape. Get that / camera out of my face.

SARAH *tries to move out of the way.* REG *can't move quickly enough.*

ALICE *enters. She spots* SARAH *and is momentarily star-struck.*

ELSA. Think of it as publicity.

ELSA *puts her hand on* SARAH*'s shoulder.*

SARAH. Get your hands off me.

SARAH *pushes* ELSA.

IAN *tries to stop* SARAH.

ALICE. Excuse me.

ELSA. She pushed me.

SARAH. What are you going to do about it?

IAN. Everybody calm down.

ALICE. Excuse me?

ELSA. Not everybody – she.

ALICE. Excuse me?

SARAH. What? I want to be edited / out of that.

ALICE. Are you Doctor O'Toole?

ELSA. Did you get that on camera? She pushed me.

REG. In close-up.

SARAH. Yes. Yes I am.

Turn that red light off.

REG. Stay back. Expensive equipment here.

ALICE. Could I have your autograph? (*She thrusts a bit of paper and a pen at* SARAH.)

ELSA. Ian? Face this way a bit.

IAN. Turn the camera off.

SARAH. No problem. And who will I . . . ?

ALICE. Alice.

You're very good. I don't watch much TV – but I like that show.

What will happen with you and the anaesthetist?

MAGGIE *enters with guitar. She looks like a Brazilian model/hooker.*

She starts setting up. ZOË *follows.*

IAN. Sarah – just go. That's the best.

SARAH. Ah now – that would be telling.

Alice, you wouldn't have a knife anywhere, would you?

Any kind?

ALICE. Let's see.

ZOË (*coming towards them*). She's just beginning.

SARAH. You?

ZOË. You?

IAN. Could we at least keep the noise down?

SARAH. What is this?

REG. A nightmare?

IAN. I really think you should leave.

ALICE *finds a butter knife.*

SARAH. You do, do you? Well – fuck off. I'm not leaving.

ALICE. Will this do?

IAN. What are you going to do?

Butter us to death?

MAGGIE *plays the intro to 'Only Love Can Break Your Heart' (Neil Young).*

ZOË. Yes, just leave, you B-list soap person.

ALICE. Am I in an episode?

MAGGIE *sings over the following.*

SARAH (*to* ZOË). Shut your face, you trout.

ALICE. I suppose everyone gets fifteen minutes.

SARAH *takes out an apple from her bag.*

SARAH. See, I have an apple. I am cutting it with a butter knife.

ELSA. Are you getting this, Reg?

IAN. Don't do it, Sarah.

   SARAH *hacks at the apple with the butter knife.*

SARAH. HA HA HA HA HA HA HA. Watch me.

ZOË. You're deranged.

SARAH. You can talk.

IAN. She's being dramatic.

ALICE. Do I have any lines?

IAN. Put the knife down, Sarah.

ALICE. Do I get paid?

SARAH. This is the kind of thing that stops you from sleeping.

ZOË. Fishwife. Call the police.

ALICE. Is this really an episode?

IAN. I think about you all the time.

ELSA, ZOË *and* ALICE. What?

SARAH. Not a day goes by when I don't think of you.

IAN. Does he please you – more than I do?

   Do you call his name out?

SARAH. Ian – don't. Don't.

IAN. Your black hair still clogs the plughole.

ALICE. Up the revolution.

SARAH. You've got to get Draino.

ELSA. This is the war we all understand. Have you got that, Reg?

   NEIL *enters.*

ALICE. This is my favourite episode.

MAGGIE. Daddy?

SARAH, ZOË *and* ELSA. Neil.

SARAH. I thought you were . . .

NEIL. I came back to hear Maggie sing.

I wanted to hear you sing.

IAN. Oh hello. Look over there.

NEIL. What?

MAGGIE. You made it, Daddy.

IAN *decks* NEIL. *There is uproar. Everybody piles in.*

MAGGIE *changes tack. She plays a loud grating intro to 'You Made Me Gay' (Gravy Train).*

Sings.

Your cock ain't nothing anyway
I'd rather suck a dog off
And I'll just use a cucumber to get my fucking rocks off
Maybe I should change my ways and only stick to Ladies
Cos I hate shitty menz and I don't want shitty babies.
Gravy train, you made me gay.

Everyone is quiet.

Are we all sitting comfortably?

She reverts to the former song and sings a verse and chorus of 'Only Love Can Break Your Heart'.

NEIL. That's beautiful.

End.

Stella Feehily interviews Paul Cunningham

PAUL CUNNINGHAM is an award-winning correspondent, presenter and author with RTE, Ireland's national TV and radio station. He has reported extensively from conflicts in Northern Ireland, Lebanon, Bosnia, Kosovo, Algeria, Afghanisatan, Sudan and, most recently, Nepal. He also has reported on the fall of the Berlin Wall, emergence of Poland from Communism, and on natural disasters in Mozambique and the United States.

SF: *Darfur. Who is killing who and why?*

PC: The killing, rape and destruction can be mainly laid at the door of the Government of Sudan and its militia, the Janjaweed, who brutally responded to the emergence of armed separatists in Darfur in early 2003. Despite the Khartoum Government's strong denials, it's broadly accepted that its military forces supplied arms to the Janjaweed and supported its operations from the air and the ground. However, more recently, the armed opposition groups have been securing more land by the gun in order to strengthen their position at the faltering peace talks. Aid agencies are increasingly critical of Darfur's rebels because their activities interrupt the aid effort.

Who are the Janjaweed?

Arab nomads who, for generations, have herded their camels and other livestock through western Sudan. In recent decades, they've become increasingly involved in clashes with landed African farmers as the Sahara expands and pasture decreases. Many African farmers felt disenfranchised from the Arab-dominated Government in Khartoum. When some African farmers took up an armed struggle in 2003, the Arab Government used the Arab Janjaweed to fight their war for them. However, not all farmers support separation and, similarly, not all nomads have been engaged in blood-curdling activity. But it's fair to say that as the Arab Government increasingly supported the Janjaweed, the landed farmers increasingly defined themselves as African. So, as a result of the conflict, the muddy generalisation has become effectively true.

You were out there on several occasions in 2004. What did you see?

Again and again, cameraman Michael Cassidy and I came across empty burnt-out villages, and camps filled with people telling horrific stories of rape and murder. It was impossible to corroborate them, but there was a consistency to what we were told: after being bombed from the air, the Janjaweed forced everyone out. We met representatives of the Government, army, rebels, victims and an unexpected encounter with a hundred heavily armed Janjaweed, kitted out with the latest satellite phones, returning from an encounter with the rebels. They were herding hundreds of camels which they had stolen from farmers.

Is the situation in Darfur less dangerous for civilians than it was a year ago?

Only because most farmers have already been burnt out and now reside in camps. There are two million living under canvas. Women still live under fear of rape – every day they have to collect firewood and leave themselves open to attack. That said, peace talks are underway and the Government is attending. One of the main rebel groups, the Sudanese Liberation Movement, splintered in mid-2005 and this caused major difficulties. At the time of writing, the stated hope of US negotiators is for a deal on a political way forward by the end of 2005. However, agreeing a deal is one thing. Implementation is another.

How do you protect yourself emotionally, in such a situation as Dafur, when surrounded by human suffering?

In a hostile environment, your thoughts are usually totally focused on the same questions: Where do I need to go? How can I get there safely? What are the elements of today's report? Who can I get to talk? How can I get back and make the deadline for filing the story? Safety aside, you don't focus on yourself – not least because the people on the ground are in a much worse situation. It's hard to feel sorry for yourself when talking to people who've had loved ones butchered or have been violently assaulted. Journalists and aid workers are extremely privileged – if you don't like it, you can go home. Rattle a gin and tonic in a nice glass and drink your horror away. On a two- or three-week assignment, there isn't free time anyway. But there is an impact, and media employers are aware of it. Most now offer 'hostile-environment training', and counselling is available on return. However, most correspondents don't usually want to talk to medical professionals afterwards. They just try to forget it. There are high-profile cases of media workers who've turned to alcohol and drugs and that's a real issue. Some colleagues are able to see an interview only as a 'soundbite' rather than as evidence from a person who has experienced horror. When the interview is over, the person who gave it effectively ceases to exist to the journalist. This compartmentalising may be effective in protecting yourself, but has the danger of disconnecting you from the people you meet.

You were in Darfur during some of the worst violence in 2004. How do you know when a story is finished for you?

The first assignment involved travelling for two weeks and filing two-minute reports for daily news bulletins. The second time I was working on a longer segment for our current affairs programme. One was high-pressured on a daily basis, the other more difficult intellectually. Since then, I've been to Nepal to report on the Maoist rebels' fight with the monarchy; I covered the New Orleans flood; and I'm about to report on a UN Conference on Climate Change in Montreal. Next year is the 20th anniversary of Chernobyl. What does this mean for Sudan as a story? Well, unless there is a big change – peace or huge increase in conflict – I probably won't be returning any time soon. My station does not have the resources to send out personnel and, at the same time, status quo is a hard story to sell to an editor. The first question usually is, 'What's new?' It's hard to drum up interest in ongoing misery.

You also work as an environment correspondent. Is it difficult to come back and focus on environmental issues after reporting on the extremes of human misery?

Coming back to domestic life can be difficult. Sometimes it can seem like you are leaving something 'important' only to return to meaningless conversations about property, holidays and good schools. People may be interested in your assignment but usually only for a few minutes. It's easy to get disconnected. Yet, after a few days, you usually re-adjust. Work piles up and you have to get back into the swing of it. Now I find foreign assignments invigorating because, on many occasions, it links the policy decision of the west with global impacts. For example, Darfur was of interest to me not just because of the scale of the human tragedy but also because its genesis was, in part, environmental. The Sahara has been increasing in size and reducing the amount of pasture. This in turn led to increasing conflict between the nomads and farmers. Extreme weather conditions will become more common as a result of global warming.

How do you create these story opportunities?

All reporters have interests and there is an expectation that such interests will be translated into proposals. However, there is usually a political dimension – does my idea cross the patch of another correspondent? Pitching an idea therefore involves several aspects: knowledge of story, ability to sell it in a pithy proposal and avoiding conflict with other reporters. With international stories, you need a clear financial appraisal too.

How do you pitch a story to a news editor?

News editors have a set of criteria: 'What's new about the story?' 'Is it important?' 'Who does it affect?' 'What are the wider implications?' They are snowed under with requests for coverage and so have to be brutal: 'We heard that last week!' 'Same old stuff he or she always says!' 'How many times can we cover the dangers of illegal dumping?' etc. etc. Selling a story is an art – suggest it in as few words as possible, press it with maximum effect but prepare yourself for the drop.

Can you describe the workings of a news organisation such as RTE? How do you think it differs from that of say ITN or the BBC?

The difference came into sharp reality when working in Mozambique during the horrific flooding a few years ago. I met a BBC correspondent who was part of a team comprising a producer, driver, translator, cameraman and a helicopter! And they had three similar news teams in the field! And separate teams for radio! Whereas we can usually only have one correspondent in the field with a cameraman or - woman, and we are expected to cover all radio demands as well. At times of major international stories, we operate with two teams. For example in Kosovo, we had one team in Belgrade for the NATO bombing while my colleague Tony Connelly and I reported on the exodus of Albanian refugees into Macedonia and Albania. Coming from a small country with a colonial past, like Ireland, can often open doors as you can be viewed as less of a threat. And that's known. Many of my RTE colleagues have heard of 'Irish' journalists in the field who then turned out to be anything but.

Camaraderie plays a big role in your work – especially in the conflict zones. What's your experience of this?

My father was concerned when I told him I wanted to be a journalist because it was known to be difficult to get into and also had a reputation. His question was: 'Do you want to be hanging around in bars all day?' To me it sounded very attractive! In domestic news, the day of 'Lunchtime O'Booze' is long gone. Twenty-four-hour radio and television has put paid to that. There are usually two types of conflict situations – one is where you are roughing it and there isn't an opportunity to go crazy, the other is where hacks are based in a hotel and travel out to get stories. In the latter case, there are opportunities for wild times but mostly people are working to so many deadlines that parties are few and far between. Anthony Lloyd's book on Bosnia, *My War Gone By: I Miss It So*, brilliantly shows how crazy it can get – but that's rare. Camaraderie is certainly evident – often we will form a small team and go to places together. If any media worker gets into trouble then the rest of the 'pack' will certainly help. But there is also rivalry – Irish viewers can watch all the British channels and so we strive to be as good, if not better, than the BBC, ITN or Sky.

'No sane or rational person keeps returning to sites of conflict and/or warfare.' A psychologist talking about the work of a foreign correspondent made that statement. Does it ring true?

Michael Herr's book on Vietnam, *Dispatches*, is, in my view, the best insight into conflict and its impact on journalists. However, the days when journalists were given free access to war are long gone. Now the buzzword is 'embedded' where reporters travel with armies and have to put up with restriction and censorship. Different times, different risks. According to the International Federation of Journalists, 1,200 media workers have been killed in the last twelve years. Sometimes they were targeted for a story. Sometimes they were killed just because of their profession. Sometimes they were in the wrong place at the wrong time. In all cases, they were driven by a desire to inform and, usually, expose something that powerful people wanted to remain hidden. Most reporters realise the tremendous power that they have: the ability to inform millions of people that something is important. There is also the glory that goes with getting to a conflict first or closer than anyone else. The trick is to balance such demands with safety concerns. The media workers most at risk are local reporters who have to live in a place after a story is published or freelance journalists who feel the need to go further than anyone else to ensure their stories sell.

The 'adrenalin rush' is frequently mentioned in biographies of foreign correspondents, male and female, and people spoke to me about it during my research interviews. What is it about?

There is undeniably a rush associated with this line of work. Covering Sudan for the first time was a case in point – we mostly operated within a twenty-five-mile radius of one town in Darfur. Given that the country is the size of France, it would be impossible for us to say that we recorded history per se. While there were certainly risks – abduction, landmines and danger of firefights – we didn't have any near-death experiences. Then, just as we were leaving to return to the airport, we literally drove into a contingent of heavily armed Janjaweed, with the latest satellite phones, herding hundreds of camels across the Sahara rim. We got our footage, made our way out of the country and ran the exclusive shots. A week later, a long time in television terms, our images were used as a colossal backdrop by BBC's *Newsnight* programme. There was most certainly a rush in the desert and deep satisfaction back at home!

Has becoming a father changed your approach?

Yes. I'm more careful about what I do. My focus has also become more orientated towards the impacts of war on families and children. I appreciate more what's often taken for granted. The change, however, was gradual rather than immediate and started when I met my partner, Flor MacCarthy.

Immigration at Record High

The total immigration flow into Ireland in the twelve months to April 2005 is estimated at 70,000 – the highest figure on record since the present series of annual migration estimates began in 1987. The estimated number of emigrants in the same period was 16,600, resulting in a net migration figure of 53,400, compared with 31,600 in the twelve months to April 2004.

The natural increase in the population (i.e., births less deaths) for the year ending April 2005 was 33,500. The combined effect of the natural increase and migration was a population increase of 87,000 (+2.2 per cent), bringing the population to 4.13 million in April 2005.

The main features of the 2005 figures are:

- The April 2005 population is the highest since the census of 1861 when the census for that year recorded a population of 4.4 million.
- The excess of births over deaths has more than doubled from 16,600 in the twelve-month period ending April 1994 to 33,500 in the corresponding period to April 2005.
- Over a third of immigrants (38 per cent) were nationals of the 10 new EU accession states, which joined the EU on 1May 2004.
- 17 per cent of immigrants are from Poland while 9 per cent are from Lithuania.
- Emigration is at its lowest level (16,600) since the series began in 1987.
- 45 per cent of emigrants went to countries other than the EU and the USA, while nearly one quarter (24 per cent) of all immigrants originated from outside the EU and USA.
- The age profile of emigrants was younger than that for immigrants. Half of all emigrants were aged 15-24 years, while just over half (54 per cent) of all immigrants were aged 25-44 years.

Published 14 September 2005 by the Central Statistics Office, Ireland: http://www.cso.ie

A Nick Hern Book

O go my Man first published in 2006 as a paperback original by
Nick Hern Books, 14 Larden Road, London W3 7ST, in
association with Out of Joint and the Royal Court Theatre

O go my Man copyright © 2006 Stella Feehily

Stella Feehily has asserted her right to be identified as
the author of this work

Front cover photograph: Iain Lanyon, www.keanlanyon.com

Typeset by Country Setting, Kingsdown, Kent, CT14 8ES
Printed in Great Britain by Bookmarque, Croydon, Surrey

A CIP catalogue record for this book is available from
the British Library

ISBN-13   978 1 85459 907 0
ISBN-10   1 85459 907 0